BILL
SEVERN'S
MAGIC
WORKSHO

BILL SEVERN'S MAGIC WORKSHOP

ILLUSTRATED BY

CRAVEN & EVANS /
CREATIVE GRAPHICS

HENRY Z. WALCK, INC.
New York

Library of Congress Cataloging in Publication Data
Severn, William.
    Bill Severn's Magic workshop.

    Includes index.
    SUMMARY: Step-by-step instructions for making and using a
variety of props and devices in more than sixty magic tricks.
    1. Conjuring. 2. Tricks. [1. Magic tricks]
I. Craven & Evans/Creative Graphics. II. Title.
III. Title: Magic workshop.
GV1547.S49   793.8   74-25981
ISBN 0-8098-3535-5

MANUFACTURED IN THE UNITED STATES OF AMERICA

Designed by Jacques Chazaud

10 9 8 7 6 5 4 3 2

CONTENTS

INTRODUCTION

Magic has grown into a worldwide hobby of all kinds of people of all ages not only because they enjoy performing but also because of the creative fun it provides in the making and trying out of new tricks.

The twenty-five projects in this magic workshop and the more than sixty tricks explained for the use of the props and devices that are to be made should give the do-it-yourself hobbyist a whole closetful of magic to combine the fun of both making and doing.

But hopefully this book will do more than that by explaining some of the basic principles that will inspire the reader to make his own magic out of all sorts of readily available materials and out of his own personality. It is intended as an experimental workshop in the performance as well as in the construction of magic.

All the projects can be put together without the need for special tools, skills, or expensive equipment—with such things as a pair of scissors, a kitchen can opener, adhesive tape. Simple step-by-step directions are given for making each prop, along with detailed instructions for tricks, for their presentation, and suggestions for inventing others.

There are easily made trick cards and coins, ways to turn tin cans into magic tubes and canisters, to convert cardboard boxes, cartons, and other things into utility apparatus. Some are intended for public performance and others for the close-up entertainment of just a few friends. All are based on tested principles of professional magic and have been constructed and tried in performance according to the directions given.

But magic, like all theatrical crafts, is highly individual. What works well for one magician may not suit the performing style of another. The props and methods of magic, like the scenery, costumes, and make-up of the stage, are merely devices for creating illusion. Each performer must discover for himself what will or will not work for him and his own best way of doing things.

It is in that sense that this workshop is intended to be experimental—a starting place for each individual to discover some of the fun of going his own way in magic.

BILL
SEVERN'S
MAGIC
WORKSHOP

1

CARDS
AND TAPES

THE LONG ONE

When someone chooses a card and returns it to the pack, so
it seems lost among the others, this "locator" will let you cut
the cards right to it and quickly bring the chosen one to the
top. It has other uses for controlling cards in the pack and is
very easily made.

What you need:

A pack of cards, scissors, and a roll of transparent tape,
the non-shiny kind such as is marketed under the trade
name of Magic Tape. (Shiny tape will reflect light and give
the trick away.)

How you make it:

Take any card and put it face up on a table. Tear off a
length of the tape the width of the card. Stick the top half of
the tape across the entire bottom end of the card. Then turn
the card over so it is face down. Bend the tape up to fasten
it across the end of the back of the card, but attach it so that

1

the fold of the tape comes just below the card's bottom edge. This has the effect of lengthening the card a tiny fraction of an inch. Finally, trim the ends of the tape with the scissors to round off the corners. You should now have a card that will stick out slightly from all the rest when it is placed in the pack.

The set-up:

Have that locator card on the bottom of the face-down pack. The taped end should be toward you when you are holding the pack.

How you use it:

Spread the pack with both hands and ask someone to choose a card. While he is looking at it, square up the pack and take it in your left hand. Cut the pack by drawing about half the cards off the bottom and dropping them on top. That places the locator somewhere near the center.

When the chooser is ready to return his card, bring your right hand, palm down, over the pack, fingers in front and thumb to the rear. Feel for the locator and lift it with all the cards above it; open the pack there so he can put back his card. Then drop your cards back on top. His card appears to be lost in the pack, but it is right under the locator.

Give the pack two or three genuine cuts by lifting batches of cards off the top and putting them at the bottom, and then cut again at the locator. Lift it with all the cards above and put them at the bottom. The chosen card is now on top of the pack.

Multiple Choice

Instead of having just one card chosen, you can have several people choose cards and still control them. After the first card has been chosen and you have brought it to the top, spread out the pack for someone else to take a card. Cut the pack to bring the locator to the center as before and then open the pack there for the second person to return his card. That automatically puts the second chosen card right on top of the first one. Cut them to the top and repeat the same thing with a third person. A final cut at the locator will leave all three chosen cards on top of the pack.

Controlling Groups of Cards

You can also use the locator to keep arranged groups of cards together. For example, start with the locator on the bottom of the pack and the four Aces on top. Cut the pack a few times by lifting batches off the top and putting them on the bottom. Then cut at the locator, lifting it and all the cards above, and put them at the bottom. The four Aces will be right back on top again.

Cutting the Aces

If you want to make a trick of that, cut the pack a few times and bring the four Aces to the top. Deal off the first one and turn it face up on the table. Cut the pack a few more times and deal off the second Ace and turn it up. Cut again, deal another, and so on, until you have dealt out all four in what appears to be a skillful display of your ability to cut the pack to an Ace each time.

You can set up a winning poker hand, or any other group of cards, and control them the same way. Here are some other tricks you can do with The Long One:

THE LONG ONE

Strip of non-shiny tape
fastened to face of card

Tape
folded under
to back of
card

Stuck to back
so there is
tiny margin below
bottom edge

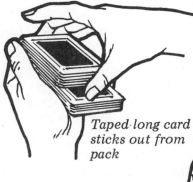

Taped long card
sticks out from
pack

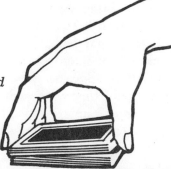

Cutting
the pack

The Nose Knows

This humorous way of revealing a chosen card usually gets a good laugh. Have a card chosen and use the locator to bring it to the top of the pack. Take the pack in your right hand between your thumb at one side and fingers at the other and hold it upright with its back toward you.

Bring the pack up in front of your face and press the rear card, the chosen one, against the tip of your nose. Explain that you are trying to get a picture of the chosen card in your mind. With the rear card pressed to your nose, draw the pack downward half its length. The chosen card will seem to rise right up out of the pack in front of your forehead.

Card at Any Number

Use the locator to bring a chosen card to the top. Ask the chooser to call out any number from one to twenty. Hold the pack in your left hand and deal the cards singly, face down, into your right hand, putting each card down on top of the one before as you count aloud to the number the person called.

Turn that card face up to show it to him and say, "I want you to be convinced that your card is not now at that number. This is not the card you chose, is it?" When he agrees that it isn't his, turn it face down, slide it in among the ones you have counted, and put them all back on top of the pack.

The counting has reversed the order of the cards so the chosen one, which was on top at the start, is now at the number he called. Say that you intend to make his card jump from wherever it may be in the pack to exactly the number he gave you. Riffle the pack and then deal the cards off as you count them aloud again. When you reach the number he called, turn that card face up and show him it is the one he chose.

Behind Your Back

As easy as this is to do, it may gain you credit for some clever sleight of hand. Have a card chosen and use the locator to bring it to the top. Then hold the pack behind your back with both hands. Ask the person what card he chose and when he tells you, say, "I can't see any of the cards, but I'm going to try to find that one card in the pack, take it out and turn it face up, and then push it back in among the others."

Riffle the cards behind your back and make a few sounds with them so it will seem that you are doing something difficult. Then simply take the top card, turn it face up, and push it back among the rest. Bring the pack out from behind your back and spread the cards to show him his chosen card face up among the others.

Mind Spell

This one uses the locator as a sort of place marker in the pack to keep arranged cards in order so you can spell out the name of a mentally chosen card and turn that card face up on the last letter you spell.

Set it up by putting these five cards on top of the pack, in order from the top down: King of Clubs, Jack of Hearts, Queen of Spades, Four of Diamonds, Eight of Diamonds. Turn the pack *face up* and take off ten cards. Put the locator face up on the pack and the ten cards face up on that. Keep the arranged pack in its case until you are ready to show the trick.

"I'll deal you a poker hand of five cards," you tell someone, "but we're not going to play poker. This is a mental spelling bee." From the top of the face-down pack, deal five cards, one at a time, in a row across the table. Turn them face up and ask him to think of any one of the cards. "Just choose one mentally," you say. "Don't tell me which one you have in mind."

Pick up the cards *in the same order as you dealt them out* and put them back on top of the pack. Cut the pack several times by lifting batches off the top and putting them on the bottom "to mix up the cards." This puts the locator and the ten that were beneath it on top of the five that were stacked. Finally, cut the pack at the locator, lift it off with all the cards above it, and put them on the bottom.

The cards are now set, from the top down, to automatically spell out any one of the five you first showed him, because the number of letters in the name of each card matches the number of cards that are above it. Ask the person what card he has in mind. Suppose it is the Four of Diamonds. Spell the name aloud, dealing one card off the pack for each letter you spell: "F-o-u-r o-f D-i-a-m-o-n-d-s." Turn the last card face up and show him that you have spelled right to it.

A Simple Force

Here is how the long card is used to force a card—to get someone to take the card you want him to take. Start with the card you intend to force on top of the pack and The Long One on the bottom. Bring them together in the pack by giving it a few genuine cuts, lifting batches off the top and putting them on the bottom. Finish the cuts with the long card and force card near the center.

Then lift off the long card and all the cards above it. Keep that pile in your right hand and gesture with it toward the squared-up lower pile in your left hand as you hold it out to the person and say, "Will you please take a card?"

If you do it casually, he will take the top card of the lower pile, the force card, since it is the only one offered to him. Done offhandedly, this is much less suspicious and more convincing than most tricky or elaborate methods of forcing.

When you wish to force more than one card, start with the ones you want to force in order on top of the pack. After the first person has "chosen" his card, close the pack, cut it once or twice, then lift again at the long card so the next person can take one, and so on.

Other Ways to Make the Card

Instead of lengthening the card by attaching a strip of non-shiny tape, you may prefer to use one made with two cards. With rubber cement, a glue stick, or some other adhesive, just fasten the face of one card to the back of another so that the bottom edge of the top card extends a fraction of an inch to the rear.

Another way is to cement one of the plastic collar stays from a man's shirt between two cards that are fastened squarely together, so that the rounded end of it sticks out slightly as a tab that can be gripped by your thumb. A straight-headed pin, a short length of very thin wire, a strip from a wide rubber band, or a little piece cut from another card are among things that can be cemented between two cards to provide something to grip at the back edge.

All such double-card devices for making a long card also give it double thickness, which makes it a bit easier to locate in the pack, but they are a little more obvious and more awkward to use than a single card with a taped edge.

THE RIFFLER

This is a trick card made of two cards that are detachable so that you can set it up to force any card you wish, one that a person merely peeks at in the pack, which then automatically vanishes. It is a handy magical tool, especially when used with matching duplicate cards from another pack.

What you need:

Double-stick transparent tape, the kind that is sticky on both sides.

A pencil, ruler, pair of scissors, and a nail file.

Two matching packs of cards to give you a supply of duplicates.

How you make it:

Take a Joker from one of the packs and put it face down on a table with its narrow ends top and bottom. Measure $\frac{1}{16}''$ down from its top edge and draw a light pencil line across from side to side. Cut along the line to trim off that top edge and then use the nail file to round the two top corners.

About $\frac{1}{2}''$ up from the *bottom* end of the card attach a $2''$ length of the double-stick tape across its back. Now take any other card you wish to use as a force card. Lay that face down on the back of the short card so the bottom and side edges of the two exactly meet. Press them with your thumb so the sticky tape between the two holds them together. Because they are fastened only with tape, you can peel them apart whenever you want to substitute a different card for the one at the back. That allows for a free use of matching duplicates to fit whatever trick you plan to do.

The set-up:

Turn the double card so its open end is toward the front and slide it into its pack somewhere near the center.

How you use it:

Hold the pack face down on the palm of your left hand, thumb across the back and fingers around the far side so about half the pack extends to the front beyond your hand. With your right hand, thumb on top and first and second fingers against the front edges, bend the front ends of the cards up and back toward you and then let them riffle down from your fingers by releasing pressure so the cards spring singly in quick succession. As they spring back down, the pack will break open at the short card of the stuck-together pair.

Try it a few times before a mirror and you will see that the riffled pack "breaks" almost automatically. With the right amount of pressure by your fingers, it will always open between the short card and the one stuck to the back of it. It isn't difficult to do but does take a little practice to do smoothly every time. You may find after you try it that you want to trim the short card a bit shorter by cutting a hairline more off the top edge.

Here's how to use it to force a card:

Have the Two of Diamonds, for example, stuck to the back of the short card and together with it at the center of the pack. Ask the person who is to choose the card, "Can you snap your fingers?" Have him snap them a few times and then tell him, "I want you to snap your fingers as I flick these cards before you. I'll stop the second you snap, so you can peek at that one card without touching it or removing it from the pack."

Hold the cards so you can riffle them rapidly in a steady

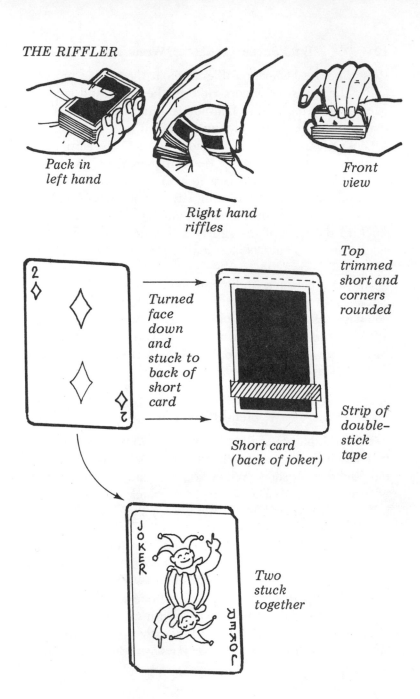

THE RIFFLER

Pack in
left hand

Right hand
riffles

Front
view

Turned
face
down
and
stuck to
back of
short
card

Top
trimmed
short and
corners
rounded

Short card
(back of joker)

Strip of
double-
stick
tape

Two
stuck
together

stream before his eyes. Riffle through them once or twice and as he snaps his fingers riffle to the break and hold the pack open at the Two of Diamonds. "Right there? Please fix that card in your mind and remember it."

Close the pack and put it aside. To make his card vanish from the pack, just pick up the cards again and hold them face up so the person can watch for his card as you deal them one at a time from your left to your right hand. He won't see the Two of Diamonds among them because it is stuck to the back of the short card which appears to be a single card with only its face showing, so that his card seems to have disappeared.

Having a person snap his fingers as you riffle through the cards is a dramatic and convincing way to force one. But if you wish, instead of having him snap his fingers, you can just ask him to call out to you to stop as you riffle through the cards. Here are some examples of the sort of tricks you can do with The Riffler:

Sleight of Foot

Take a duplicate of the card you intend to force and slide that down inside your right shoe so it goes in under your foot and doesn't show. When you are ready to do the trick, take the pack with The Riffler in it, which has a card stuck to its back that matches the one in your shoe, and riffle force that card as explained.

"You've all heard of sleight of hand," you say, "but have you ever seen anyone perform sleight of foot?" Put the pack on the floor and tap it twice with the toe of your right shoe. Then pick up the cards and say, "Believe it or not, I've sneaked your card out of the pack with my toes."

Turn the pack face up and ask the person who has "chosen" the card to watch for it as you deal them singly from hand to hand. When you finish showing through them, ask, "Did you see your card? No? You didn't see it? . . . Which one was it?"

As he names his missing card, lift your right foot and bend that leg up across your left knee to help balance yourself. Show your right hand empty and pull the matching duplicate card out of your shoe. Hold it up so everyone can see what card it is and say, "Sleight of foot!"

Stringing Along

"I've just learned a new trick that I'd like you to see," you say as you take up a pack of cards. You riffle the pack to have someone peek at one card and remember it. "Now watch—I'll just tap the cards like this and your card will jump right to the bottom of the pack." You turn the pack face up, show the bottom card, and ask if that is the chosen one. But to your seeming embarrassment, the chooser says that you are wrong. It is not his card.

"Well, it must be somewhere near the bottom," you say. "Just watch for it, please, and let me know when I come to it." You deal the cards, one at a time, face up, from hand to hand. But the person doesn't see his chosen card anywhere in the pack. "That's very strange," you say. "I don't understand how the card could disappear. I'd better read the instructions for this trick again."

You put the pack aside and remove an envelope from your pocket. Printed on the face of it in big letters is the word: INSTRUCTIONS. Opening the envelope, you take out a folded "instruction sheet," which you start to read to yourself. Then you read part of it aloud: " 'There is one card this trick won't work with. Don't ever try to do it if somebody chooses the Jack of Clubs. That card always vanishes from the pack.' "

You look up at the chooser and ask if his card happened to be the Jack of Clubs. When he says that it was, you shake your head and say, "Now they tell me." Then you look at the "instruction sheet" again and read aloud: " 'P.S.—Is this what you're looking for?' "

As you say those words, you unfold the bottom of the paper and the Jack of Clubs drops down out of it, to hang dangling at the bottom of a string.

For this, set up The Riffler to force and then vanish the Jack of Clubs. At the top of a sheet of business-size stationery type or print the words of the "instruction sheet" that you will read aloud. Fold the paper as you would a business letter, creased into a top, middle, and bottom sections. Take the duplicate Jack of Clubs from the other pack and fasten one end of a foot-long piece of soft white string to the top of the back of that card with a piece of tape. Attach the other end of the string to the paper, at the center, just below the middle fold.

Coil up the string and put it on the middle section of the paper. Lay the card on top of it. Fold the bottom of the paper up against it and then the top section down on that. On the face of an envelope, print in big letters: INSTRUCTIONS. Slide the folded paper into it and have the envelope in an inside pocket of your jacket.

Follow the presentation as given. Riffle the pack, force the Jack of Clubs, and pretend that the trick is to make the card jump to the bottom of the pack. Show the bottom card and act embarrassed when it turns out not to be the chosen card. Quickly deal the face-up cards one at a time from your left hand to your right, showing them as you run through the entire pack. Because the Jack of Clubs is stuck to the back of the short card, the chooser does not see it anywhere in the pack.

Admit that you had better read the instructions for the

trick again. Remove the envelope, take out the folded paper, and put the envelope aside. *Open only the top fold of the paper,* holding the bottom of it closed with your thumb. Read aloud from it. Ask if the chosen card happened to be the Jack of Clubs. Then read from it again, unfold the bottom of the paper, and let the duplicate Jack of Clubs fall out, dangling from the end of the string. Hold the card with your fingers so the audience can see that it is the missing Jack of Clubs.

Three Times One Is Nothing

Three people in turn peek at a card in the pack. Then they all claim to have seen the same card—the Ace of Spades. But you prove that they never saw the card at all because it isn't anywhere in the pack. Where it is, as you show them, is up your sleeve!

To set it up, attach the Ace of Spades to the short card of The Riffler and have it somewhere near the center of the pack. Fasten a wide, flat rubber band around your left arm and slide a duplicate Ace of Spades under the rubber band so it will be hidden up your sleeve.

With The Riffler, force each of three persons in turn to look at the Ace of Spades. Stand back so you are facing all three and raise your hand as you tell them, "When I count to three, I want you all to call out the names of the cards you peeked at in the pack." Count aloud to three, drop your hand as a signal, and they will all call out, "Ace of Spades!"

Shake your head and say, "You all thought you saw the same card? Perhaps you suspect that all the cards in the pack are Aces? I wouldn't try to fool you that way. . . . Honestly, I wouldn't." Turn the pack face out, holding it with your left hand in front of your waist, and deal the cards one at a time off the face of the pack into your right hand, to show them all as you run through the pack. "As a matter of fact, there isn't a single Ace of Spades anywhere in the deck."

Put the pack aside and say, "If you think your eyes have been playing tricks on you, they certainly have." Show your right hand empty and reach up inside your left sleeve to pull out the duplicate Ace of Spades and display it. "Because the Ace of Spades is the one card I always keep up my sleeve!"

FLIP FLAPS

Here are several trick cards with flaps that flip. The flaps are parts of cards, or full cards, hinged with tape to other cards so they can be swung from front to back. With the first one you can instantly and almost visibly change one card to another.

Flip Top

You deal a card from the pack and put the pack aside. The card is shown to be the Jack of Spades, for instance, but as you turn it over to show the back and then take it from your hand it suddenly changes to the Four of Hearts. Both the full face and back of the apparently single card may be shown.

What you need:
A pack of cards.
Non-shiny transparent tape.
A pair of scissors.

How you make it:
Any two cards may be used, but for explanation we'll use the Jack of Spades and Four of Hearts. Cut the Jack of

Spades in half across the middle and discard the bottom half. Cut another ¼″ off the bottom edge of the top half so that you have slightly less than half a card.

Put the Four of Hearts face up on a table with its narrow ends top and bottom. Turn the piece of the Jack of Spades face down so that its top end, with the rounded corners, is at the bottom. Place it on the table right above the top end of the Four of Hearts so they almost touch but with enough space between them so they can be hinged together.

Hinge them by running a strip of the non-shiny tape across from side to side and then turn the whole thing over and attach a matching strip of tape to the other side to reinforce the hinge. Fold them together so the flap of the Jack of Spades is face up against the face of the Four of Hearts and trim off any excess tape at the sides of the hinge to round off the corners.

The set-up:
Have the trick card face down, with its taped end to the front, on top of the pack.

How you use it:
Deal the card face down into your right hand and put the pack aside. Lift your hand so the back of it is toward the audience and your fingers point to the left. With your other hand, pull the card up far enough to show it to the audience as the Jack of Spades, call attention to it, and then push it back down again.

Hold it as it is with your right hand. Bring your left hand down to the bottom edge of the card. Take that edge between your left thumb at the front and first finger at the rear and lift it straight up to the top, opening the card out on its hinge, as if you were opening a suitcase by lifting the lid. Put your right thumb against the hinge so the card is

held upright above your hand. To the audience it appears
that you have turned the card up to show the entire back of
it. The attached flap piece remains hidden inside your right
hand.

Display it that way for a moment. Then bring your left
hand up to take the card. From the rear, put your left first
finger against the face of it. Push down and forward and
grip the card between that finger and thumb. As the flap
goes to the back, pull the card free from your right hand. It
has suddenly changed from the Jack of Spades to the Four
of Hearts.

Hold the flap pressed to the back with your thumb and
show both sides of the card. Then pick up the pack with
your right hand, put the card on the bottom, and drop the
pack into your pocket.

Back Flip

You can use the same sort of a flip flap to change the color
of the back of a card—say, from red to blue—instead of the
face of it. Two cards with the same faces but with backs of
different colors are needed. They should have backs with a
white border, not an overall pattern that extends to the
edges. Let's say they are both the Two of Spades, one
red-backed and the other blue-backed.

Cut the red-backed Two of Spades in half, discard the
bottom piece, and trim a little more off the bottom edge of
the remaining piece so that you have slightly less than half a
card. Turn it face up with its rounded corners toward the
bottom. Put the blue-backed card face down on the table
and hinge the half-card to its top edge with tape, as before,
reinforcing the other side of the hinge and trimming it to
round off the corners.

Fold the flap face down against the back of the face-down

blue card. Turn the pack face up and put the trick card face up on top. Then deal it off the face-up pack and handle it as you did the two-faced flip card, but by first showing it as a red-backed card and changing it to blue.

Full Flip

With this, you can show the full face and back of a card, instantly change it to another card, and again show the full face and back. In place of a half-card, a full card is used as a flap, hinged to the side of another card instead of to the top.

Let's say you use an Ace of Spades and a King of Diamonds. Turn the Ace face down and the King face up on a table. Bring them together side by side so the left-side edge of the face-up King is exactly opposite and almost touching the right-side edge of the face-down Ace. Hinge their side edges together by running a strip of the non-shiny tape from top to bottom. Turn them over, reinforce the hinge with another strip of tape, and fold them together so the face of the Ace comes against the back of the King.

The set-up:
Put the trick card face down on top of the pack with its open side to the left and then turn the pack face up so as to keep the card flat beneath it and not reveal its double edges.

How you use it:
Pick up the pack, turn it face down so the open side of the trick card is to the left, and deal the card off into your right hand, pressing your thumb lightly on the back of the card to keep it closed. Put the pack aside.

With your right hand, show the face and back of the King of Diamonds. Hold your left hand with its back toward the audience, fingers to the right and slightly cupped in toward

FLIP FLAPS

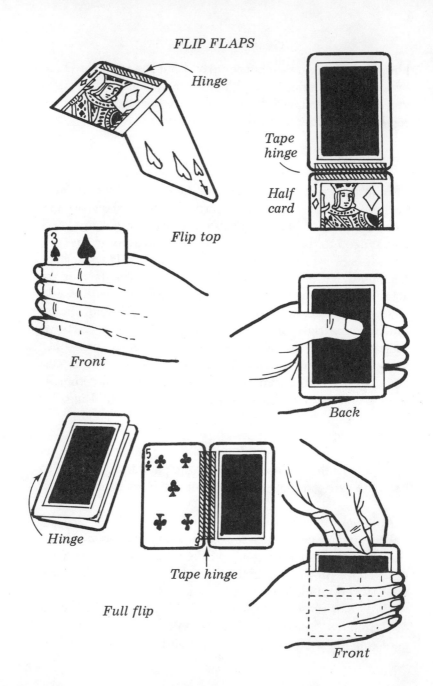

Hinge

Tape hinge

Half card

Flip top

Front

Back

Hinge

Tape hinge

Full flip

Front

you. With your right hand, turn the card sidewise so its hinge is at the top. Transfer it to your left hand by placing the face of the sidewise card against your left palm and fingers so the card is entirely within your hand. Hold it there between the inner tips of your left fingers and the base of your thumb.

Now lift the card open on its hinge by gripping the bottom edge of the rear part between your right first finger and thumb and bringing it straight up to the top, and hold it there with your left thumb to display the back of the card to the audience. The other card, hinged to its side, remains concealed within your left hand.

Bring your right hand over to take the card. From the rear, put the tips of your fingers against the upright part and bend it down and outward over the top of your left hand, gripping the hinge between your fingers and thumb to lift the entire card away from your left hand. Suddenly it has changed from the King of Diamonds to the Ace of Spades. Show the front and back of it, pick up the pack and put the card on top, and put the pack away.

Double Change

With a Full Flip card, as with the other flip flaps, you can change the color of the back from red to blue, instead of the face. Make it by hinging a face-down red-backed Ace of Spades side by side to a face-up blue-backed Ace of Spades.

You can also work a double change, for example to change a red-backed Four of Clubs to a blue-backed Eight of Spades. Make that by hinging a face-down blue-backed Four of Clubs to the side of a face-up red-backed Eight of Spades. Then fold them together so the face of the Eight comes against the back of the Four. Show the double card as a red-backed Four, handle it the same way as the ordinary Full Flip card, and show the change to a blue-backed Eight.

After a while the hinges of any of the flip flap cards will need replacement because frequent handling tears them. But it is a simple matter to peel off the old tape and rehinge them.

PASTEBOARD ACROBATS

One of these cards whirls around at your fingertips. The other floats through the air—in two directions. The first is hardly a trick in itself since it takes only a few seconds to show, but it is an amusing and rather startling little surprise to use with other card tricks.

The Twister

You pick up a card, tap it with your finger, and it suddenly whirls around like a pinwheel, spinning first one direction and then the other before it comes to rest again in your hand.

What you need:
Two cards.
Rubber cement, a glue stick, or other adhesive.
Flesh-colored cloth adhesive tape, ½" wide.
Fine-gauge copper wire or other thin wire.
Wire snips or an old pair of scissors.

How you make it:
Cut off a 2" length of wire. Make a small hole in the center of one of the cards for the wire to go through. Hold the card with its narrow ends top and bottom. From the back of it, push about 1" of wire through the hole. Bend

that part of the wire down flat against the face of the card. Leave the remainder of the wire sticking out at a right angle to the back of the card.

Fasten the bent-down end of wire to the face of the card with a small strip of the cloth tape. Coat the face of that card and the back of the other card with adhesive, stick them squarely together so all edges meet, and allow the adhesive to dry. Wind a small strip of cloth tape tightly around the wire that sticks straight out from the back.

The set-up:

Where you put this trick card depends on how you want to introduce it into a card routine. It could be in your pocket, in a small basket on your table into which you have put cards from some other trick, or face down on top of a pack that is hidden behind something on your table.

How you use it:

This should be presented offhandedly, not as magic really intended to fool anybody but as something that just happens, seemingly to your own surprise, as you pick up one of the cards.

Hold the card at the extreme left corner between the first finger and thumb of your left hand with your other fingers drawn back out of the way. Lift that hand high directly in front of you.

Bring your right hand up behind the card and snap your finger against it to call attention to it. Touch your right first finger to the top edge of the card with that hand palm downward. Keep that finger where it is and grip the little wire handle that sticks out from the back of the card between your thumb and the side of your second finger.

Roll the handle between them to rotate the card to the right, then reverse it and spin it around to the left. Do it

Wire goes through
center—front end
is bent flat and
taped down

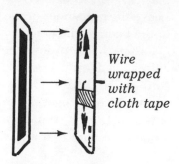

Wire
wrapped
with
cloth tape

Second card
cemented to
face of first

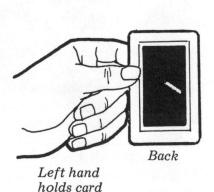

Back

Left hand
holds card

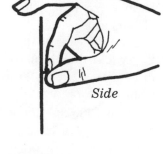

Side

Right first
finger taps top—
second finger
and thumb grip
knob

rapidly just once in each direction. Then take the card again, as at the start, between your left thumb and finger and immediately drop your right hand to your side. Toss the card into a basket or put it away in your pocket.

The Two-way Floater

The Queen of Hearts or any card floats horizontally through the air from the pack in your left hand to your waiting right hand. Placed back on the pack, it then rises vertically, to float up through the air to your hand above it.

Based on a trick at least a half-century old, this has been simplified in the handling, and the final rise through the air with the same card has been added. It is *not* a close-up trick and should be performed a little distance from those who are watching.

What you need:
A spool of strong, black thread with a dull finish.
A fairly large sewing needle to make holes in one of the cards.
Non-shiny transparent tape.
A pair of scissors.
Two cards, one of which should be a Queen of Hearts if you are going to use the presentation that follows, but otherwise any two.

How you make it:
For explanation, we'll call the Queen of Hearts the "floater" and the other card the "anchor." With the needle, make two holes in the floater, directly opposite each other, one about ½" in from the right side and the other the same distance from the left side, both about ¼" down from the

top of the card. Enlarge the holes slightly by working the needle around in them.

Cut about 2½′ of thread from the spool. (After you try the trick you may decide you want a longer or shorter thread.) Hold the floater card face down. Take one end of the thread and push it *up* from beneath the card through the hole at the right and then bring it across the back of the card to thread it *down* through the hole at the left. Draw through about a foot of that end of the thread and lay that card on the table for a moment.

Put the anchor card face down on the table to the left of the floater. Take the *same end* of the thread and fasten it to the center of the back of the anchor card. Do that by laying the thread horizontally across the card, sticking a vertical strip of tape over it, tying the thread, and then putting another piece of tape over the knot to hold it firmly.

Now take the floater card and slide it to the right on the table until you draw almost all the length of thread through its holes, but leave enough of the free end for fastening and tying. Do that by bringing the free end of the thread around the right-side edge of the floater card to the back. Attach that free end to the back of the floater by taping it down, then knotting it, and finally covering it with another piece of tape.

The set-up:

Hold the anchor card face down in your left hand. With your right hand, draw the floater card as far to the right as the thread will allow. Fold the thread that is between the two cards loosely on the back of the anchor card. Put the floater card face down on top of it and hold the two together. Draw up a little of the thread that comes through the two holes at the top of the floater so that a small loop of it is left there.

Put the two cards face down together on top of the pack and slide the pack into its case until you are ready to use it.

How you use it:

Remove the face-down pack from its case with the threaded cards on top. Discard the case and hold the pack upright, narrow ends top and bottom, in your left hand.

Bring your right hand to the pack. With your right first finger and thumb, grip the thread that comes out through the two holes of the top card, the floater. Draw out enough of a loop so you can hook your right second finger down through it. Keeping your finger hooked through the loop, move your right hand, palm down, to the right until the thread is taut.

Release the floater from your left hand and the top of the pack. Slowly draw your hands apart and the card will float across through the air from the pack and come directly under the first finger of your right hand, which you lift a little to take it.

Keep your right hand in that position, holding the card between your first and second fingers. Move your thumb out to the left, forward and then up, to hook it under the thread that is stretched across from your left to your right hand. With the thread hooked over your thumb, put the floater back on the pack in your left hand. Hold the card on the pack with your left thumb and then lift your right second finger out of the loop.

Hold your right hand, palm down, directly above the pack, with the thread still hooked over your right thumb. With your left hand, release the floater from the back of the pack. Draw your right hand upward and the card will float up through the air to that hand above it. Catch the card with your fingers, show it, and put it back on the pack.

Here are two routines for presenting the effect:

THE TWO-WAY FLOATER

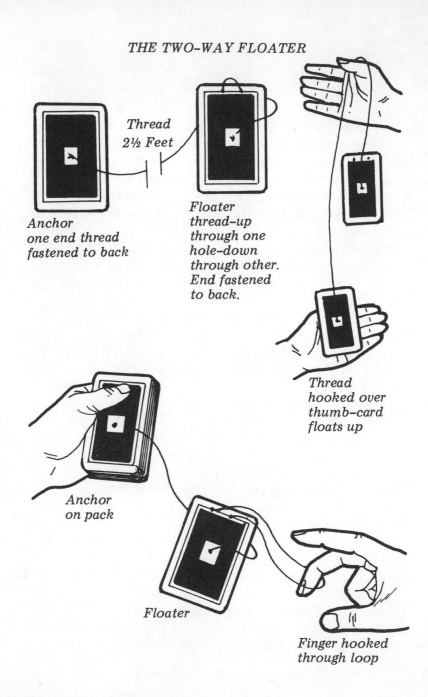

Anchor
one end thread
fastened to back

Thread
2½ Feet

Floater
thread-up
through one
hole-down
through other.
End fastened
to back.

Thread
hooked over
thumb-card
floats up

Anchor
on pack

Floater

Finger hooked
through loop

The First Woman Astronaut

With the Queen of Hearts as the floater, you remove the pack from its case and say, "Did you know that history's first woman astronaut was the Queen of Hearts? She began floating through the air hundreds of years ago, long before there was atomic power or space capsules or rockets to the moon. At least, there's an old legend that the Queen was the first to fly and that even at her age she still likes to swoop around once in a while."

Hold the pack in your left hand. With your right second finger hooked through the thread, move your hand out to the right. "I didn't believe it—until one night when I was playing cards with some of my friends," you say. "I needed a Queen to win—and the old girl came floating right out of the pack to my hand." Float the Queen of Hearts across and then put it back on the pack. "But none of my friends saw it. They were all busy looking at their own cards. And when I told them—well, I mean . . . it *is* pretty hard to believe." With your thumb hooked under the thread, lift your hand above the pack, float the card up to it, and shake your head as you say, "Sometimes I wonder if it ever really happened at all."

I'll Do It Again—Visibly

For this, you need a second pack of cards with backs of a different color. Let's say your floater pack is red-backed and the other one blue-backed. Make up The Riffler, as explained earlier in this chapter, to force and then vanish a Queen of Hearts from the blue-backed pack. With the red-backed one set up to float its Queen of Hearts, have both packs on your table. You pretend to explain how a trick is done and at the end leave the audience more puzzled than ever.

"Magicians never show how their tricks are done," you say, "but tonight I'll make an exception to that rule. I'll run through a trick first the way I usually do it—with these cards with the blue backs."

Have someone "choose" the Queen of Hearts from the blue pack by peeking at it as you riffle them. Then hold the pack in your left hand, with your right hand out to the side, just as if you were making the card float across. "What I'm doing," you say, "is magically extracting the card from the pack, so it floats right out of it and over to my other hand. Then I secretly tuck it away in my pocket." Put your empty right hand into your pocket as though you were putting away a card and then bring your hand out again. "Of course you didn't see any of that because the magic was invisible. But your card really has vanished from the pack."

Ask the person which card he peeked at and then show through the blue Riffler pack so he can confirm the fact to the audience that the Queen of Hearts has vanished. Drop that pack into your pocket and return to your table.

"This time I'll do it again with these cards that have red backs," you explain as you take up the other pack. "As you'll see, red gives the whole thing much more visibility." Open the red case, remove the pack, and hold it ready to perform the floater. "Let's assume that someone has chosen a card. Which one was it? Oh, yes—the Queen of Hearts. What I did was . . . simply this. . . ."

Float the Queen from the pack across to your right hand. "With the red cards, you can all see it, can't you?" Put the card back on the pack and then make it rise up through the air to your other hand as you smile and say, "Now that you know exactly how it was done, please don't tell anybody."

THE ANTI-GRAVITY CARDS

You deal a number of cards from the pack and spread them out, one at a time, on the palm of your hand. Suddenly you turn your hand over, so the cards face the floor, and they all cling to your hand without falling.

In this simplified close-up version of what has been a favorite stage trick of many magicians, one faked card does the work. The others are arranged so the trick card "locks" them into place.

What you need:
A pack of cards.
A roll of transparent tape.

How you make it:
Put one of the cards face down on a table with its narrow ends top and bottom. Take a strip of tape about 2½″ long. Fold the tape at the center with its two sticky surfaces toward the inside. Press the center fold so the tape sticks together for about ½″. Then separate the two bottom ends and bend each of those ends outward. Stick those two ends firmly to the back of the card at its center.

You should now have a tent-shaped tab of tape that stands straight up from the back of the card. But because it is flexible it will also bend flat when the trick card is stacked with others in the pack.

Put your left hand, palm down, on top of the card so the tab slides between your second and third fingers. Press those knuckles together and grip the tape between the sides of them. With the tape gripped that way, lift your hand and the card will seem to cling to it.

Now keep the card gripped as it is and turn your hand palm upward. Take a few more cards from the pack and slide them, one at a time, under the sides of the trick card so they come between it and your fingers. Turn your hand over and all of them will hold there. Basically that is how the trick card is used. But when you perform, the cards are arranged in a special order, not haphazardly, so that more of them will stay in place.

The set-up:
Turn the pack face up, add the trick card to the face of it, and slip the pack into its case. Have that in a jacket pocket.

How you use it:
Remove the pack, discard the case, and hold the cards face up in your left hand. Deal about fifteen cards, one at a time, into your right hand and put aside the remainder of the pack. Dealing them reverses the order, so the trick card is now at the bottom of the batch in your right hand.

Hold your left hand outstretched, palm upward. Rest the face-up cards together on your left palm, narrow ends top and bottom, so the tab of tape slides between your second and third fingers. Grip the tab tightly between the sides of those knuckles and keep it gripped that way until the end of the trick.

Take the top face-up card with your right hand, turn it sidewise, and slide it under the front of all the cards on your left hand until it touches the tape. Take the next card and, without turning it, slide it under the right side of the others. The third card goes sidewise under the rear of the others. The fourth, without turning, goes under the left side.

With the trick card, those four "lock" all the rest of the cards in place. The rest are added, one at a time, by sliding them in under the first four, moving around in clockwise order.

When you have them all in place, keep the tab gripped

THE ANTI-GRAVITY CARDS

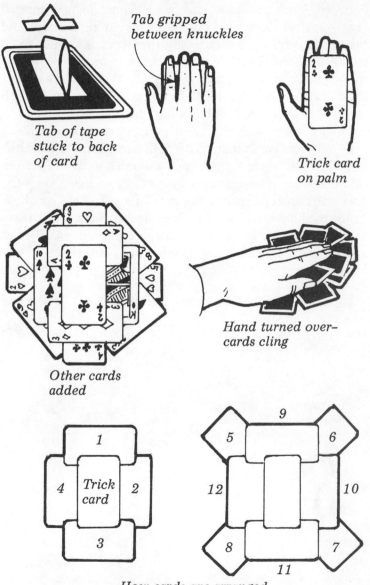

Tab gripped
between knuckles

Tab of tape
stuck to back
of card

Trick card
on palm

Other cards
added

Hand turned over—
cards cling

	1	
4	Trick card	2
	3	

How cards are arranged
to "lock" them in place

between your knuckles and press your fingers upward gently against the spread cards. Snap your right finger and thumb. Slowly and dramatically turn your left hand palm downward and hold it that way a moment with the spread-out cards clinging to your hand. Then bring your left hand up toward your face and gently fan yourself with them, as if you were holding a big fan.

Finally, turn your left hand palm upward again. Bring your right hand over to it. With both hands, bunch the cards together and square them as you release the tab from between your left fingers. As you straighten them, keep the trick card on top. Spread the cards face up between both hands to show them, square them again, and replace them on the remainder of the face-up pack. Slide them all back into the card case and drop it into your pocket.

2

❧ ❧

TIN CAN
TRICKERY

A SIMPLE CHANGING CANISTER

You drop a red rubber ball into a gleaming metal canister
and put on the lid. A moment later, the ball has changed
into yards and yards of red ribbon—or perhaps the ball has
changed into an egg, a lemon, or a handkerchief. This
simple utility device will allow you to change almost any
object that will fit inside the canister for anything else
previously hidden in it.

What you need:

An empty tin can about 4½″ tall and 3¼″ in diameter, the
standard size used for many fruits and vegetables.

A kitchen can opener that will cut cleanly and leave no
rough edges.

Two identical colored plastic lids to fit the top and
bottom of the can, such as those available in supermarkets
as "pet-food covers" for preserving food in an opened can.
(Such plastic lids also are supplied with some varieties of
canned goods.)

A piece of stiff cardboard, large enough to cut a circle from it the diameter of the can.

Cloth adhesive tape, any color, 1" wide.

Self-adhesive decorative paper, the kind pressed into place to decorate closet shelves, table tops, walls, and other areas. This should be black or some solid dark color.

A pencil and a pair of scissors.

How you make it:

Remove both the top and bottom of the can with the can opener and cut around the edges again if necessary to make sure they are smooth. Peel off and discard the outside paper label. Thoroughly wash and dry the can.

Rest the can on the piece of cardboard and draw a pencil line around its bottom rim. Cut out the circle of cardboard. Cut four strips of cloth adhesive tape, each about 6" long. Fasten two strips to the face of the cardboard circle so their centers form a cross and their ends stick out to the sides. Turn the cardboard over and fasten the other two strips, crisscrossed, to the opposite side. Loosely roll all the ends of the tapes up on themselves to hold them out of the way.

Push the cardboard circle down inside the can to its center so it will form a flat divider there across the middle of the can. Since the cardboard is slightly larger than the circumference of the can, its edges will bend up a little, which helps to hold it in place. When you have the cardboard at the center of the can, unroll the ends of tape and fasten them to the sides of the can, up the sides above the cardboard and down the sides beneath it. Press them firmly into place inside the can. The result should be a can divided into an upper and lower compartment by the cardboard fixed across the middle of it.

Cut a strip of the black self-adhesive decorative paper about 4" long and 2" wide. Peel off the backing. Attach one end of the strip inside the can just beneath its top rim. Smooth it down along the side of the can and then across the cardboard circle to fasten the other end of the strip to the center of the circle. Cut another strip the same size and fasten it the same way, overlapping the first one slightly. Then attach another strip beside that one, and so on, until the entire inside top of the can is covered with the decorative paper.

Turn the can over and cover the other end of the inside by running similar strips of decorative paper from just beneath the rim, down the side, and across the circle to its center.

The two faces of the cardboard divider must now be covered with two large circles of the decorative paper. Rest the bottom of the can on a piece of the paper, with the backing sheet of the paper face up. Draw a circle around the bottom of the can with the pencil. Move the can over, draw another circle, and cut them out. Peel the backing from one paper circle and fasten it to the top face of the cardboard, smoothing the edges of the paper up around the inside of the can. Then turn the can over and fasten the other paper circle to that face of the cardboard.

You now have a can completely covered inside with black decorative paper and divided at the center into two compartments. Fit one of the plastic lids to the bottom of the can and its matching lid to the top.

The set-up:

For explanation, let's say you intend to change a rubber ball into a handkerchief. Remove the bottom lid, stuff a handkerchief into that compartment, replace the lid on the bottom, and rest the can on it. Have the rubber ball beside the can on your table.

How you use it:

Stand facing the audience a little to the left of the table. Pick up the can near its bottom end with your right hand. Remove the lid with your left hand and keep the lid in that hand.

With your right hand, tilt the can over forward until it is upside down. Shake it to indicate that it is empty, hold it upside down a moment, and then bring it upright again. The turning of the can gives the audience a brief glimpse at the inside of it, where the black paper covering helps to conceal the divider. Casually turning it upside down and shaking it "proves" that it is empty.

Take the can with your left hand, which also holds the lid. Pick up the ball with your right hand, display it, and put it into the can. Then take the lid and fasten it on the top. Transfer the can to your right hand, which grasps it rather loosely near the bottom, between the thumb at one side and fingers at the other.

Turn your body slightly to the right so you are almost facing the table and your body momentarily covers the view of your right hand from in front. Drop your right hand a little and simply let the can tip forward and over, bringing its bottom end to the top, as you put the can on the table.

Leave it there and walk away a few steps as you talk. Because both lids are identical, the audience should not be aware that you turned the can upside down. But the bottom end, with the handkerchief in it, is now at the top. When you are ready to show the change, pick up the can with your left hand, remove the lid, and take out the handkerchief to display it. Casually tip the can upside down once more to "prove" that it is empty and the rubber ball is no longer in it. Put the lid back on and put the can on the table.

Here are some examples of the many tricks you can do with the canister:

A SIMPLE CHANGING CANISTER

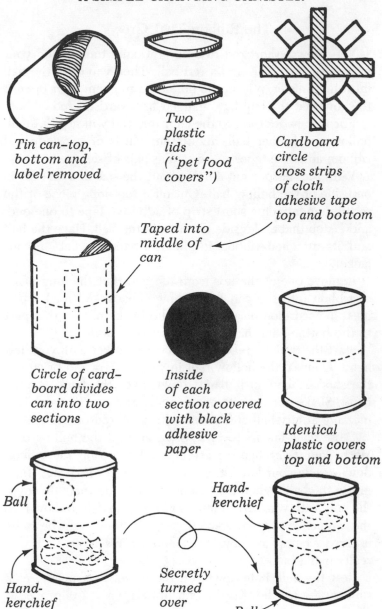

Tin can—top,
bottom and
label removed

Two
plastic
lids
("pet food
covers")

Cardboard
circle
cross strips
of cloth
adhesive tape
top and bottom

Taped into
middle of
can

Circle of card-
board divides
can into two
sections

Inside
of each
section covered
with black
adhesive
paper

Identical
plastic covers
top and bottom

Ball

Hand-
kerchief

Secretly
turned
over

Hand-
kerchief

Ball

The Ribbon That Grows

You show a short red ribbon, gradually tuck it into your hand, and change it into a red ball. Then you drop the ball into the canister, put on the lid, and a moment later open it to show that the ball has changed into yards of red ribbon.

For this, in addition to the canister, you will need a small hollow red rubber ball, about four yards of $\frac{1}{2}''$ wide red ribbon, adhesive tape, and a strong pair of scissors.

With the scissors, cut a hole about the size of a quarter in one side of the hollow ball. Cut off a foot-long piece of the red ribbon, attach a short strip of adhesive tape to one end, and fasten that end inside the hole in the ball. Have the ball and its attached ribbon in the left-hand pocket of your jacket.

Remove one of the lids from the can. Put the long piece of ribbon into the can by folding it back and forth upon itself in accordion pleats. Put the lid back on, turn that part to the bottom, and have the can on your table.

Start the trick by reaching into your pocket with your left hand. Conceal the hollow ball in your fingers and bring out the short ribbon so it hangs down over the back of your hand. Shake out the ribbon, show it, and say, "I went to a meeting at city hall and collected a little red tape."

Close your fingers to form a fist around the hollow ball. With your right hand, start gradually poking the ribbon down inside your left fist, really pushing it a little at a time inside the ball. When the ribbon is all inside the ball, cover the hole with your left thumb, and turn the ball to show it to the audience. Open your fingers so they can be seen otherwise empty and say, "Those politicians at city hall . . . really had a ball."

Rest the ball, hole down, on the table. Pick up the can, remove the top lid, tip the can upside down to "prove" it empty, and put the ball into it and replace the lid. As you turn to put the can on the table, let it tip over to reverse it and bring the bottom end to the top. Leave it on the table and move away a little.

"Politicians and magicians," you say. "Sometimes we both start with one thing and wind up with something else. Take a solid proposition like that little red ball. . . ." Point to the can, pick it up, remove the lid, and pull out a few inches of the red ribbon. "Suddenly it's all a matter of red tape again." Quickly pull out the rest of the ribbon, whirling it from the can as a long streamer, as you say, "And the red tape just grows . . . and grows . . . and grows!"

Pop Goes the Corn

You invite a boy from the audience to assist you and ask whether he likes popcorn. "Well, I have the corn," you explain. "All we need is the pop." From a paper bag, you pour some unpopped corn into a bowl. "I'll provide the corn and the magic. Do you think you can supply the pop?"

Taking up the can, you remove the lid, pour the unpopped corn into the can from the bowl, and replace the lid. You give the boy the empty paper bag and explain that you want him to blow it up and then burst it between his hands so it makes a loud "pop." As you hold the can above it, he blows up the bag and attempts to explode it.

You make the most of the comedy of having him try, but don't embarrass him if he fails. If he is finally unable to burst the bag, put it aside and ask him to puff out his cheeks instead, and to make a loud popping sound when you count to three. One way or the other, you congratulate him for being a "proper popper."

Then you open the can, pour out popped corn to fill the bowl, and invite him to taste it as you join him in sampling it. If you wish, you can use a cardboard picnic plate instead of a bowl, and give him the dish of "magic popcorn" to take back to his seat.

Set it up in advance by filling the bottom section of the can with popped corn. Fill it right to the brim so it is tightly packed under the lid and won't rattle around inside when you handle the can. Have enough unpopped corn in the paper bag to fill the other section of the can completely. Beside the can on your table, have a clear glass or plastic bowl.

Show the can empty. Pour the unpopped corn from the paper bag into the bowl. Then fill the top part of the can with the unpopped corn and put on the lid. Secretly reverse the can to bring the bottom to the top as you put it on the table. Follow the rest of the routine as given and finally pour the popped corn from the can into the bowl.

TIP-OVER TUBE

A ball dropped into the top of this tube may vanish and later reappear or change color from white to red. Rice poured into the top of the tube may change to an egg. It has other uses in combination with other props for various routines.

What you need:

Two empty small-size vegetable cans, about $3\frac{1}{4}''$ high and $2\frac{1}{2}''$ in diameter.

Black self-adhesive decorative paper.

Green cloth or plastic adhesive tape, $\frac{1}{2}''$ wide.

A pair of scissors and a ruler.

Three rubber "bouncing balls," two of which match and one that is different, such as two white and one red. They should fit easily into the cans and not show above the top rim when they are inside.

How you make it:

Wash out and dry the two empty cans. Peel off the labels. Make sure the edges where the tops have been cut away are smooth. Leave the bottoms of both cans intact.

Put one can bottom up on a table. Turn the second can bottom down and put that on top of the first one so the two bottoms exactly meet. Wind a strip of the cloth or plastic adhesive tape twice around them to fasten the two cans tightly together bottom to bottom.

From the roll of black self-adhesive paper measure off and cut two pieces, each 5″ by 6½″. Peel the backing from one and cover one side of the joined-together cans with it, from top to bottom within the rims, sticking it on a little at a time and smoothing it into place to avoid wrinkles. Then peel the backing from the second piece and apply that to the opposite outer side in the same way.

Cover the edges where the two pieces of decorative paper meet with vertical strips of the green tape, one at each side. Wind a horizontal strip of green tape around the center where the bottoms of the two cans meet. Finally wind another green strip horizontally around the top just beneath the edge of the rim, and a third strip around the bottom just above the rim.

You should have what looks like a single black tube with green stripes down its two sides and bands of green around the top, center, and bottom. It is open at the top and bottom but closed inside at the center where the bottoms of the two cans meet, divided into an upper and lower section so that anything dropped into the top will not fall all the way through and come out the bottom.

The set-up:

To try the handling of it, start with the tube empty and have one of the white balls beside it on your table.

How you use it:

Stand behind the table. Pick up the ball with your left hand, show it, put it into the top of the tube, and drop your left hand to your side. Snap your right first finger and thumb above the tube. Then grasp the tube near the bottom with your right hand, fingers at the front and thumb at the rear. Lift the tube straight up from the table and hold it there. Because the ball hasn't fallen through, it seems to have vanished from the tube.

You are still holding the tube above the table with your right hand. Quickly turn the tube over *from right to left* and bring it down on the table top so that what was the upper end of it is now at the bottom. As you turn it over upside down to rest it on the table, the rapid downward motion will keep the ball hidden in the tube so that it becomes trapped beneath it. Take your hand away, snap your fingers, grasp the tube again and lift it. The missing ball has reappeared.

That is the basic tip-over move and the simplest use of the tube. It requires a little practice so that you can do it casually and smoothly. By magician's logic, turning the tube upside down "proves" there could be no ball inside it. Yet when you lift the tube a moment later, the ball is there.

Passing Colors

To make a ball seem to change color from white to red as it is dropped through the tube, start with a red ball hidden in the top section and a white ball beside the tube on the table.

THE TIP OVER TUBE

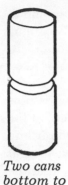

Two cans
bottom to
bottom

Cloth tape
banded
around
to join
cans to-
gether

Covered
outside
with black
decorative
paper

Green
bands

Green
stripe

Looks
like
single
black
tube

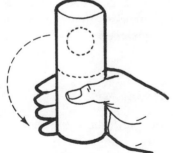

Hidden ball
in top–tube
grasped at
bottom

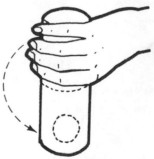

Turned over from
right to left to
bring ball to
bottom

Stand behind the table and grasp the tube near the bottom with your right hand, fingers in front and thumb at the rear. Lift the tube straight up to show there is nothing under it. Then turn the tube upside down from right to left, as explained, and bring it to rest on the table again. Keep your right hand as it is, still holding the tube.

The red ball that was hidden in the top section is now beneath the bottom of the tube that covers it. Pick up the white ball from the table with your left hand, drop it into the top of the tube, and immediately lift the tube straight up with your right hand so that the red ball rolls out at the bottom. It looks as if the ball changed from white to red as it passed through the tube.

That leaves the white ball hidden in the top section. With your right hand, turn the tube over again as before and put it down on the table so the white ball is trapped under it at the bottom. Pick up the red ball with your left hand, drop it into the top, and with your right hand immediately lift the tube to show that the red ball has changed back to white.

Here's a brief routine of quick surprises in which a ball seems to fly back and forth between your pocket and the tube:

Here, There, and Where?

Both white balls are used for this, although you seem to prove to the audience that you are using only one. Start with one hidden under the tube and the other in view on the table.

Pick up the ball from the table with your left hand and show it. Grasp the tube near the bottom with your right hand as your left hand drops the ball into the top of it. Immediately lift the tube with your right hand to let the other ball roll out the bottom.

It looks as if you dropped a ball right through the tube from top to bottom, thus "proving" convincingly that there could be nothing else inside the tube and that the ball freely passed through it. With your right hand, turn the tube over from right to left and rest it on the table with the duplicate ball now concealed under it.

Show the visible ball with your left hand and openly put it into your jacket pocket. Brush your hands together so the audience is convinced that you really left the ball in your pocket. Grasp the tube with your right hand, lift it up, and reveal that the ball has flown from your pocket to reappear under the tube. Rest the tube on the table beside the ball.

Pick up the ball with your right hand and toss it to the left hand. Catch it, show it, and drop it onto the top of the tube. Snap your fingers over the tube and then snap them again in front of your pocket. Lift the tube to show that the ball has vanished from under it and reach into your pocket and bring it out.

As you replace the tube on the table, turn it over from right to left to bring the hidden ball inside it to the bottom again. With your left hand, drop the ball you took from your pocket into the top of the tube and immediately lift the tube with your right hand so the other one rolls out, thus "proving" again that only one ball was used.

Egg Foo Rice

This is an example of the way the tube can be combined with other props. In addition to the tube, it makes use of the Simple Changing Canister previously explained. You will also need rice, a glass bowl, a small rubber or thick cloth mat, and two identical white plastic eggs, the sort sold at toy counters. If those are not readily available, you can substitute two real eggs that look alike, but hard-boil them so they won't break and make a mess.

The plot of the trick is that rice is poured into the tube and an egg is put into the canister. When you lift the tube, the rice has changed into an egg, and when you open the canister, the egg that was put into it has vanished and you pour out the missing rice.

Set it up by filling one compartment of the canister to the brim with rice. Put on the lid, turn the canister over, put one of the eggs into the other side, and cover it with the other lid. Have the canister at the left of your table when you stand behind it.

Hide the duplicate egg in the top part of the tube. Put the tube on the mat at the right side of your table. (The mat is needed under it to deaden the sound when you later turn the tube over and the egg hidden in it comes into contact with the table top.) Pour some rice into the bowl and have the bowl at the center of the table.

"A little mystery from the Orient," you announce as you stand behind the table. "It came to me from the Orient by way of a Chinese restaurant."

Grasp the tube near the bottom with your right hand, fingers in front and thumb at the rear. Lift it to show nothing under it, quickly turn it over from right to left, and replace it upside down on the mat with the hidden egg beneath it. Leave it there, pick up the canister, and step forward with it to the front and left of the table. Remove the lid from the top of the canister and take out the other egg.

"This started out to be Egg Foo Yong, but this egg has been around so long that . . . it's not young anymore," you say, as you show the egg and then turn the canister upside down to "prove" that it is empty. "That's one reason I've decided to call this mystery . . . Egg Foo Rice."

Put the egg into the top of the canister, put on the lid, and as you turn to rest the canister on the table and your hand is concealed by the turning of your body, reverse the canister so the section with the rice hidden in it is now at the top.

Pick up the bowl, scoop a handful of rice from it, and let it pour from your hand back into the bowl. "Here's the rice." Scoop another handful, hold your hand above the tube, and pour the rice into the top of the tube. Continue to pour handfuls of rice into the tube until the top part is about three-quarters full. "Rice is the one thing you always get with every Chinese meal."

Move to the back of the table again so there is a clear view of it from the front and put down the bowl. Point first to the tube and then to the canister as you say, "The rice . . . and the egg. And now . . . Egg Foo Rice."

Snap your fingers and lift the tube straight up to reveal that the rice has vanished from it and the egg is under it. Pick up the egg and show it and put down the tube and leave it there. Place the egg on the table and take up the canister. Open it and slowly pour rice from it down into the bowl, gradually tipping the canister over until it is empty.

DROP-THROUGH PRODUCTION TUBES

You show two tubes empty and drop one through the other as further proof that there is nothing inside them. Then you reach into the stacked-together tubes and produce handkerchiefs, cups of liquid, yards of paper streamers, or whatever else you wish to conjure up from them.

What you need:
A large fruit juice can, about 7" high and 4¼" in diameter.

A coffee can, about 5½" high and 4" in diameter.

A vegetable can, about 4½" high and 3¼" in diameter.

A paper clip.

Decorative self-adhesive paper in a solid color.

Cloth adhesive tape, ¾" wide.

Scissors, a ruler, and a can opener.

Whatever items you intend to produce from the tubes.

How you make it:

Remove the tops and bottoms of the two larger cans and remove the top of the smallest can but leave its bottom intact. Make sure they are all cleanly cut open with no rough edges. Peel off the labels and wash out and dry the cans.

Open out the paper clip and bend it with your fingers into a straight upright wire except for the last loop at the bottom. Leave that loop of the clip as it is. Hold the center of the wire against the first finger of your left hand and bend it down over that finger until the entire clip forms a hook something like an "S" hook.

Cut off a 2" length of the cloth adhesive tape. Put the center of it, sticky side down, against the wire hook so that the tape comes *between* the little loop at the bottom and the upright shank. Fasten the tape and that part of the wire to the inside of the smallest can just beneath the can's top rim. Cut another 2" length of tape and cover the first strip with it to anchor the end loop of wire between the two strips and against the inside top of the can.

You should now have the bottom end of the wire firmly fastened just inside the top rim, with a straight shank of wire extending above the can for about ¾" to the point where it bends down and out as a hook.

The next step is to decorate the outsides of the other two cans. Start with the larger one. Measure off and cut a 7½" by 13½" piece of the self-adhesive decorative paper. Put the can on its side on a table, peel a few inches of the backing from the paper, and stick one end of it to the outside of the can. Slowly work the paper into place around the can, smoothing it down and peeling away the backing as you turn the can.

Trim off the excess paper at the top and bottom rims, but do not fold any of the paper over the rims to the inside of the can. The inside of the top and bottom rims must be left uncovered so there is plain metal there, to allow for freely sliding the cans through one another and to help disguise the use of the plain metal hook.

Measure and cut a second piece of the decorative paper, 6" by 13", to decorate the outside of the other large can in a similar way. Trim off the excess at the top and bottom rims, but again be careful not to bend any of the paper over the rims to the inside.

The two large cans decorated with paper are the tubes the audience will see. The smallest can, with the hook attached, is the "load can" into which you will load the things you intend to produce. It is never seen by the audience.

The set-up:

For now, to understand how the tubes are handled, just stuff a pocket handkerchief or a tissue into the load can. Hang that can inside the smaller of the two tubes by putting its hook over the top rim. Turn that side of the tube to the rear. Have that tube at the left side of your table when you stand behind it and the larger tube at the right side.

How you use it:

Pick up the larger tube with your right hand. Tilt it up so the audience can look through the bottom and see that it is

DROP THROUGH PRODUCTION TUBES

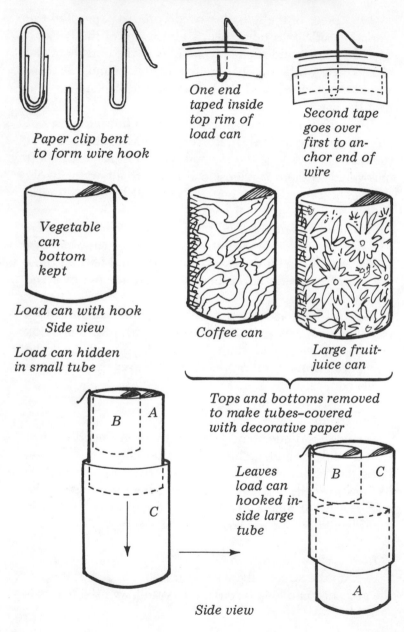

Paper clip bent to form wire hook

One end taped inside top rim of load can

Second tape goes over first to anchor end of wire

Vegetable can bottom kept

Load can with hook
Side view

Load can hidden in small tube

Coffee can

Large fruit-juice can

Tops and bottoms removed to make tubes–covered with decorative paper

Leaves load can hooked inside large tube

B   *A*

C

B   *C*

A

Side view

empty and then put it back where it was on the table. Lift the other smaller tube straight up and drop it down inside the larger one. The hook of the load can will catch over the rim of the larger tube, automatically transferring it from inside one tube to the other. Immediately lift the larger tube straight up off the smaller one and put it down on the table beside it. The load can is now hanging hidden inside the larger tube.

Lift up the smaller tube so the audience can look through the bottom of that and see that it is empty. Then put the smaller one back on the table. You have shown both tubes empty and passed one through the other as further proof that there is nothing inside them.

Take the larger tube by its top rim with your fingers inside and thumb at the rear. Press your thumb against the wire hook to hold it flat against the outside of the tube and slide that larger tube down over the smaller one so the two are nested together on the table. Leave them there, say your "magic words," and then reach into the top of the tubes and pull out the handkerchief.

Two-handed Drop Through

You may prefer this method of showing the tubes empty, by holding both of them in your hands while you stand away from the table. It speeds up the handling for a quicker and more surprising effect, but takes practice to do smoothly.

Start with the load can hanging hidden inside the smaller tube, which should be held near its center with your right hand, fingers in front and thumb at the rear. Your left hand holds the larger tube near the bottom, fingers in front and thumb at the rear. Holding a tube in each hand, stand facing the audience.

With your left hand, hold up the larger tube so the

audience can look through the bottom and see that it is empty. Turn it upright again, hold it about waist high, and move your little finger in under the bottom of the tube. Bring your right hand directly above it and let the smaller tube drop down inside the larger one. Just bring it up, drop it, and let it fall. It doesn't fall all the way through the larger tube because your little finger stops it momentarily at the bottom.

Quickly bring your right hand down under the two tubes. Draw back your left little finger to release the smaller tube so it does fall through. As the smaller one falls, catch it with your right hand and immediately hold it up so the audience can look through the bottom of that tube. Then turn the smaller one upright, bring it up underneath the larger one, and slide it up inside until the two are together. Rest their bottoms on the palm of your left hand, reach into the top with your right hand, and start producing things.

Your left little finger should delay the fall of the smaller tube through the larger one only an instant, just long enough for your right hand to come to the bottom and catch it as it falls through. The whole thing should look as if you merely showed the larger tube empty, dropped the smaller one through it, caught it and showed it empty, and then put the two together.

What to Produce

The load can will hold ten 18″ square silk or compressible rayon handkerchiefs of various colors. To load the handkerchiefs, start by folding one of them into the bottom of the can, back and forth upon itself in loose accordion pleats, until you come to the last corner. Wind that several times around a corner of a second one, then fold that into the can on top of the first, and so on. Twisting their corners together as you load them will make it much easier to pull them out individually when you produce them. The last handkerchief loaded should be packed tightly over the others and tucked down at the sides to hold them all in place so they won't pop up into view prematurely.

Instead of the usual handkerchiefs, you might produce strings of inexpensive colored beads, an array of "medals" made by hanging colored cardboard discs from loops of ribbon attached to safety pins, or a number of small bells of various tones that you can shake and ring as you take them out one at a time.

Here are some other ways you can use the tubes:

Easy Liquid Production

You show the tubes empty, put them together, reach into the top and remove four paper cups, one at a time. Then you pick up the first cup, hold it above, and pour colored liquid down from it into each of the other cups.

The liquid is water, colored to make it more visible with a few drops of kitchen food coloring. Milk may be used if you prefer, but don't use any carbonated soft drink because it is likely to fizz over while you are handling the tubes.

You will need four paper cups, colored ones that are not transparent and that have smooth sides with no handles, each about 3½″ high and 3″ in diameter at the top. No lids or other covering devices are necessary. Simply stack three of them together, pour colored liquid into the fourth cup until it is about three-quarters full, and put that one inside the others. Then put the stack of them into the load can and have it hooked inside the smaller tube.

For this production use the first method that was explained for showing the tubes empty, by keeping them on the table, not the method of dropping them through while you hold them in your hands. After you have shown them empty and nested the two together on the table, reach into the top, put your fingers inside the cup with liquid in it and ease it up a little until you can grip it between your fingers and thumb, and then bring the cup out and put it on the table. Produce the other cups, one at a time, and line them in a row. Take the first cup, hold it above the others, and slowly pour some of the liquid down into each of them.

The Magic Party

"Let's have a party," you say, as you quickly show the tubes empty, put them together, rest them on the table, and produce a paper party hat that you open out and put on your head. In rapid succession, you then produce two or three small paper coils that unwind as you spin them out, a little horn and a whistle that you sound, one of those blow-out party toys that flaps when you blow through it, and finally yards and yards of a colored crepe-paper streamer.

All the items are available at party-goods counters in most variety stores. You will need a standard crepe-paper streamer, the kind usually used as a garland to stretch across the ceiling from one side of a large room to the other for party decoration. These generally are about 2″ wide and 12 yards long.

Put the roll on a table, unwind a little of the streamer, and begin folding it back and forth upon itself flatly in accordion pleats, each about 3″ long. Don't wind it around or wrap it, just fold back and forth, creasing down the folds as you go. When you have the streamer all folded into a flat, small bundle, attach a small strip of cloth tape to the end of it, so you can later find that end without fumbling.

Put the folded streamer into the bottom of the load can.

On top of it, put one of the party blow-outs that uncoils into a flapping tube when you blow through it, then a small whistle and the sounding device from the end of a paper party horn. Next put in a few thin colored-paper throw-out coils. The party hat should be the tissue-paper kind, not one reinforced with cardboard. Open it out and put it on your head to loosen the folds, then refold it and put that into the load can on top of the other things, and tuck it down at the sides to hold everything in place.

Show the tubes empty, put them together, and take out the hat and put it on. The other things should be produced rapidly to lead to the climax of spinning out yards of the paper streamer. Throw out the coils so they unwind high in the air with flashes of color. Blow the horn, drop it to the table, take out the whistle and blow it and drop it, quickly blow through the blow-out toy and flap it, then pull out the long streamer, spinning it around and around as you whirl it up from the tubes.

CRUSH AWAY GLASS AND LIQUID

You fill a glass with red liquid from a container, cover the glass with a paper napkin, and hold the covered glass so the full shape of it can be seen within the napkin. Suddenly you crush the napkin flat between your hands, crumple it into a small ball, and toss it aside. The glass and liquid have vanished.

What you need:

A medium-size vegetable can, about $4\frac{3}{4}''$ high and $2\frac{5}{8}''$ in diameter.

A small tuna fish can, about $1\frac{1}{2}''$ high and $2\frac{5}{8}''$ in diameter.

A transparent glass small enough to fit easily inside the

larger can, such as a "cheese glass" or the footed kind in which ready-serve shrimp cocktails are packaged. It should be about 4″ high and a little less than 2½″ in diameter.

Cloth adhesive tape, any color.

Black self-adhesive decorative paper.

A 3″ by 5″ office index file card.

Double-stick (sticky both sides) transparent tape.

A large "dinner-size" 3-ply white paper napkin, about 17″ square.

Red vegetable food coloring.

A cup of water.

A small wastebasket to have on the floor beside your table.

Scissors, a pencil, and a ruler.

How you make it:

Remove the tops of both cans but leave the bottoms intact. Make sure the edges are cleanly cut, wash out the cans, and dry them. Turn the large can bottom up on a table. Put the small can bottom down on top of it, so the two are bottom to bottom, and bind them tightly together by winding a strip of cloth tape around the joined bottom rims.

Measure off and cut a 9″ by 6¾″ piece of the self-adhesive black decorative paper. Cover the outside surface of the joined cans with it by peeling off the backing a little at a time and smoothing the paper into place. Trim off the excess paper at the top and bottom rims.

Put the office index file card on a table, place the top rim of the glass upside down on the center of it, and pencil a circle around the rim. Cut out the circle and stick a small strip of the double-stick transparent tape horizontally across it. Open out the paper napkin and fasten the circle of thin cardboard to the center of it by sticking the tape firmly to the napkin. Mix a few drops of the vegetable food coloring into the water to color it red.

The set-up:

Turn the container so the small can is at the top and stand it near the rear of your table to the right. Put the glass to the left of it. Pour enough of the red liquid into the glass to fill it about three-quarters full and then empty the glass into the top of the container and dry the glass. (For later performances, you can measure out the right amount of liquid in advance and carry it in a screw-topped jar or small bottle with the rest of your props.)

Open out the napkin and place it, fully opened, in front of the container and the glass on your table. Now take the rear edge of the napkin and fold it forward a little, so that you can quickly pick it up by that edge.

How you use it:

Stand behind the table and pick up the glass with your left hand and the container with your right hand. Slowly pour the liquid into the glass by tilting the container from right to left so as not to expose the hollow bottom of it to front view. Tilt the container upright again and keep it in your right hand.

With your left hand, put the glass on the table. Then take the napkin by its rear edge and draw it back toward you to cover the glass, so the cardboard circle fastened under the center of the napkin is on top of the glass.

Now bring your left hand, palm down, over it and gently grip the rim of the cardboard through the napkin as if you were gripping the top of the glass. Leave the glass on the table where it is, but lift the cardboard about an inch and then move your hand forward. This draws the napkin off the glass, but the audience can't see the glass because the slightly lifted napkin curtains the view of it from in front.

As you lift the napkin forward with your left hand, bring the container in your right hand down behind the napkin. Put the bottom of the container over the glass and leave the container on the table. The glass is now hidden under the container, but it looks as though you are holding the glass under the napkin with your other hand.

Move out in front of the table. Your left hand is still holding the rim of the cardboard circle so that it seems to be holding the glass covered by the napkin. Bring your right hand to the napkin just beneath your left hand and close your right thumb and fingers loosely around the center of the napkin as if you were taking hold of the glass. Draw your right hand downward a few inches and take your left hand away from the top of the napkin and drop that arm to your side.

Because of the stiffness of the paper, the napkin will remain standing straight up from your right hand as if you were holding the bottom of the glass through the napkin. It keeps its round shape because of the cardboard circle at the top. Hold it that way a moment. Then bring your left hand up and suddenly crush the napkin down into your right hand to flatten it.

Crumple up the napkin with your hands and wad it into a tight ball, crushing the thin cardboard disc inside it. Take it in your left hand, toss it up into the air and catch it with your right hand, then drop it into the wastebasket beside your table.

(For other performances all you have to replace is the napkin and the little cardboard disc.)

CRUSH AWAY GLASS AND LIQUID

Small
tuna
fish
can

Fruit
can

Bottom
to bottom

Taped
together

Bottomless
container

Top
part
holds
liq-
uid

Double-stick
tape

Cardboard
circle cut
from file
card

Cardboard circle
fastened to
center of
paper napkin

Napkin, glass
and container
on table

Right hand
holds
container

Left hand
with napkin
hides glass
from view
as container
covers it

Glass
hidden
under
container

Left hand
holds card-
board disc-
looks like
glass in
napkin

Right
hand
shapes
napkin
beneath
disc

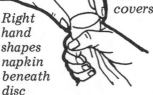

Stiff paper
napkin
stays upright

Looks like hand holds glass

SHELF AND TRAP CAN

Copper changes to silver, gold is extracted from sand, beads string themselves together, or paper clips link in a long chain with the use of this can. Whatever small things are dropped into it are trapped inside and a little shelf holds substitute objects ready to pour into your hand.

What you need:

An empty vegetable can, about 4½″ high and 3¼″ in diameter.

Poster board or other fairly stiff cardboard.

Cloth adhesive tape, 1″ wide.

Cloth double-stick adhesive tape (sticky both sides) 1″ wide.

Scissors, a ruler, and a pencil.

A small tray on which to rest the can.

Whatever items you intend to use with it as suggested in the tricks that follow.

How you make it:

Leave the bottom of the empty can intact, wash out and dry it, and peel off the label. Stand the can on the piece of poster board, pencil a circle around its bottom rim, and cut out the circle. Trim the circle slightly smaller, by cutting about ¹⁄₁₆″ from its edge all the way around. Then measure off and cut another piece of poster board that is just slightly less than 3¼″ square.

Place the circle on a table. Bend its bottom edge up to meet its top edge, crease the circle flat across the center, and then open it out halfway again so that the bottom half stands straight out at a right angle to the top half like a little shelf.

Fasten a 2½" length of the double-stick cloth tape to the back of the top half of the circle. Put the top half of the circle against the top edge of the other piece of poster board and press the two together so they are firmly fastened by the sticky tape between them.

Cut a 1" length of the *plain* cloth adhesive tape, not the double-stick tape. Attach half the tape to the front edge of the little shelf. Loosely roll the rest of that piece of tape back upon itself to keep it temporarily out of the way.

Turn the whole thing around so the back of it is toward you. Attach three 5" lengths of the plain cloth adhesive tape to the back, one across the top, one at the middle, one at the bottom. Temporarily roll up the ends of those tapes so they are out of the way.

Slide the entire piece down inside the can until it is just below the can's top rim. The shelf part should touch against the inside front of the can. Reach inside with your fingers, unroll the tape at the edge of the shelf, and fasten that to the inside of the can to hold the shelf there. Tilt the upright divider just slightly forward and fasten all its ends of tapes to the inner sides of the can by reaching in behind it from the top and bottom.

Cut two 3" lengths of tape and fasten one to each side edge of the back of the upright, running them down vertically to seal those side edges to the sides of the can. With several more short strips of tape, fastened so they overlap, seal off the edge between the little shelf and the inside of the can.

The can is handled so the inside is not shown to the audience. The mouth is always tipped back toward you. The outside of the can should be left as it is, with its plain metal finish.

The set-up:

Suppose you want to change copper to silver—pennies to quarters. Set it up by putting eight quarters inside the can so they rest on the little shelf. Turn that part of the can to the front and put it on the small tray. Have the eight pennies on the tray beside the can.

How you use it:

"One little penny," you say as you stand in back of the table and pick up one of the pennies with your right hand. Show it, hold it about a foot above the can, and drop it so it falls into the rear section, behind the divider. Pick up another penny, show it, and drop it into the can. "Two." Continue to pick them up and to drop them from above into the rear part of the can as you count aloud. "Eight little pieces of copper."

With your right hand pick up the can between your thumb at one side and your fingers at the other. Rattle the coins in it. Hold your left hand, cupped palm upward, near your waist. Swing your right hand in toward you from right to left so the back of it is to the audience. Tip the mouth of the can toward you to pour its contents into your cupped left hand. Turn the can completely upside down and then put it back on the tray, still upside down, and leave it there.

What has happened is that the pennies have remained trapped inside the can, because they slid down under the back part of it when the can was tipped, and the quarters have poured out into your hand instead. But the audience doesn't yet know that anything has happened. Apparently you have simply counted eight pennies into the can and then poured them out again into your hand.

"Eight pieces of copper," you say again as you close your fingers around the quarters hidden in your hand and jingle

SHELF AND TRAP CAN

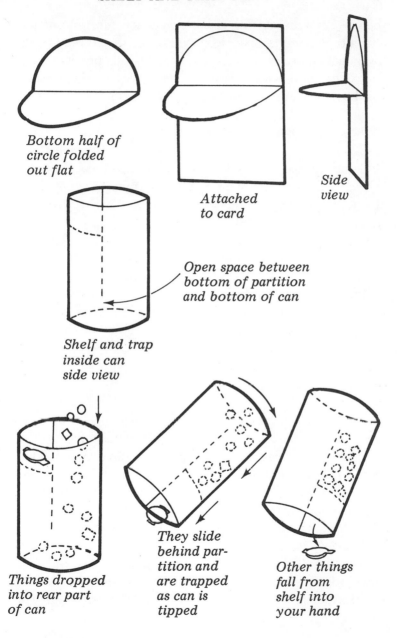

Bottom half of
circle folded
out flat

Attached
to card

Side
view

Open space between
bottom of partition
and bottom of can

Shelf and trap
inside can
side view

Things dropped
into rear part
of can

They slide
behind par-
tition and
are trapped
as can is
tipped

Other things
fall from
shelf into
your hand

them. "For hundreds of years, ever since the time of the ancient alchemists, people have tried to find a secret formula that would change base metal into precious gold and silver. But always, one ingredient seemed to be missing. Perhaps that missing ingredient was—simply a touch of magic."

Show your right hand empty. Reach into your left hand, take out one of the silver quarters, hold it up for the audience to see, and say, "Silver." Drop it to the tray. "One." Take another, show it, and continue to count them aloud as you drop them, one at a time. "Eight pieces of silver."

The reason for the tray is so that at the end of the trick you can clear your table without having to handle the upside down can again at the risk of rattling whatever is in it. Just lift away the tray with the can on it, still upside down. You also want to avoid directing any special attention to the can, because all the magic supposedly has happened in your hands.

Here are some other tricks you can do with it:

Sand to Gold

Make up three or four imitation "gold nuggets" by crumpling up pieces of gold metallic foil. Have these hidden in the shelf part of the can. With the can on its tray on your table, have a small, clear glass bowl partly filled with water and another clear bowl partly filled with sand or sifted earth. You also will need a transparent plastic sandwich bag and a paper hand towel.

Start the trick by scooping up a handful of sand and letting it pour down into its bowl. Then scoop a smaller handful and slowly trickle that down into the rear of the can from above. If some spills into the front part of the can, it makes no difference.

Pick up the can with your right hand and bring it around toward you to tip it over so the hidden "nuggets" pour into your cupped hand, which should be tilted with the back of it toward the audience. Keep them concealed in your fingers. A little of the sand may also spill out of the can, but most of it will remain trapped. Tip the can upside down and put it back on the tray to leave it there.

Dip your closed left hand into the bowl of water and wash it around as you explain that you are "washing away the dirt to pan for gold." Release the "nuggets" so they can be seen swirling in the water in the bowl and open your hand to show that the sand has all been washed away. Take out the "nuggets" and drop them into the small plastic bag so you can display them. Before going on to your next trick, dry your hands on the paper towel.

Stringing the Beads

You will need two matching inexpensive necklaces of brightly colored small beads for this, and also a drinking glass, a pair of scissors, and a spool of heavy white thread.

Unfasten the clasp of one of the necklaces so it hangs in a straight string and put that into the shelf section of the can. Cut free and remove the beads from the other string and have those in the glass. Have the scissors and spool of thread beside them on the tray with the can.

Start by showing the spool of thread and unreeling a length of it about equal to the length of the necklace. Cut it from the spool, quickly roll it into a small bundle, and drop it into the rear part of the can. The thread goes in first so the weight of the beads falling on top of it will hold it at the bottom to be trapped with them when the can is tipped.

Pick up the glass of beads, hold it above the can, and pour these down into the rear section. Rattle the can and then tip it upside down toward you and pour the necklace into your cupped left hand, but keep your hand partly closed so as not to reveal the necklace yet. Put the upside down can back on its tray.

Cup your right hand next to your left hand and shake the supposedly loose beads in your two cupped hands. Suddenly toss the necklace into the air and catch it with your left hand as it comes down. Take the other end with your right hand and hold it up to show the strung beads.

The Long Chain of Paper Clips

You will need a standard box of one hundred paper clips. Count out fifty and put those aside a moment. String the remaining fifty into a long chain of clips, by sliding them through both wire loops to attach one to another securely. Put that chain into the shelf part of the can. Dump the loose clips back into the box and close the lid. Have the. box beside the can on its tray.

Start by opening the box of clips. Hold the lid open wide. Take out two clips separately, show them, and drop them singly into the rear part of the can, as you say, "One little paper clip . . . two little paper clips . . ." Then take them out a few at a time and sprinkle them down into the can, but don't dump in the rest all at once. The audience must be convinced that they are separate. Say, "A whole lot of paper clips . . . ten, fifteen, twenty . . . I hope you're counting them with me."

Handle the can as before, tipping it over toward you so the chain pours into your left hand while the loose ones are trapped inside. Put the can aside upside down.

Shake the chain in your cupped hands as though you were

still holding loose clips. You can show it in your hands quite freely. When the chain is all bunched together it looks like a bunch of loose ones. Turn and show them in your hands to one side of the audience and then the other. Finally toss the long linked chain into the air, catch it, and hold it out between your hands.

3

❦

CONJURING
WITH CARDBOARD

THE GHOST FRAME

A small picture frame stands propped on your table, resting
on its easel-like support so the audience can look through its
front window and see that it is empty. You show both sides
and stand the frame on the table again with its back to the
audience. When you turn it around, a picture, playing card,
or something else has magically appeared in the frame.

What you need:
Three 5″ by 7″ pieces of poster board, black or whatever
color is desired.

Cloth or plastic adhesive tape, ¾″ wide, in a matching
color.

Snapshot corner mounts, the kind used to hold pictures in
an album.

Double-stick (sticky both sides) transparent tape.

A pencil, scissors, and a ruler.

A small snapshot picture, or whatever else you intend to
have appear in the frame.

How you make it:

A window opening must be cut in one of the 5″ by 7″ pieces of poster board. The opening should be 4″ wide and 5″ high. Mark it off by putting the piece on the table with its narrow edges top and bottom, then measuring 1″ down from the top, 1″ up from the bottom, and ½″ in from each side. Connect the pencil lines, cut the window, and discard the part that was cut out.

Put the three pieces of poster board in a vertical row on the table, with the window at the center and a solid piece above and below it. Separate their edges slightly, so they are about ⅛″ apart. With the cloth or plastic tape attach the bottom end of the top piece to the top end of the middle one by running a horizontal strip across to hinge them together. Then attach the bottom end of the middle piece to the top end of the bottom piece. Turn the whole thing over and reinforce the hinges with matching strips of tape at the back.

Bind off the edges of the cut-out window with strips of tape by attaching one-half the width of the tape to one side and then bending it over the cut edge to fasten it to the other side. Next bind off all the outer edges of the three pieces of poster board in the same way, by running strips of tape along them and bending it over.

Fold the attached pieces back and forth a few times so all the hinged parts are flexible and the whole thing will fold flat. Then open them out as they were at the start, in a vertical row with the window at the center. The picture, or whatever else you wish to have appear in the frame, is attached to the top section, to the upper piece of the three when they are in a vertical row.

The picture should be attached *upside down* to that part of the frame, centered there but with a clear space of about

1″ beneath the picture's bottom edge. That is to allow a margin for propping up the frame. Fasten the picture into place with corner mounts or with a short strip of double-stick tape.

Leave the section with the picture attached to it flat on the table. Bend the middle section, with the window opening, upright. Bring the third piece down behind the window, in back of it, and spread it out a little so the frame stands propped up by itself.

You are looking at the frame from the front, as the audience would be. The frame appears empty and the picture lies on the flat support behind it. Now turn the whole thing around so the back of it is toward you, which is the position it should be in when you start performing.

The set-up:

Have the propped-up frame in that position on your table, with its window to the front. The hidden picture you intend to produce is attached to the flat part of the easel as explained.

How you use it:

Stand behind your table. Call attention to the empty frame. Bring your right hand to the top of it, close the two upright pieces together, and fold them back and down on top of the flat piece so the whole thing is folded together and lies flat on the table.

With your left hand, pick up the folded frame by the end nearest to you. Keep it folded and hold it up to show the window front of it to the audience again. Bring your right hand to the bottom edge and pivot that edge straight out forward and then to the top so as to turn the whole thing end-for-end to show the audience the back of it.

Keep that back section toward the audience as it is and

with your left hand lift up the window and the piece behind it until they are at a right angle to the back. Let the frame fall open, swing the back part in toward the window, and stand the propped frame on the table again with the window toward you.

This should look as though you simply showed the front, then the back, and then propped it up to stand it on the table with its back to the audience. When you want to reveal the picture that has appeared, just turn the whole propped-up frame around, without lifting it from the table, and bring the window to the front.

Another Way to Handle It

You may prefer this way of showing the frame empty and making the picture appear, without having it propped open on your table. Set it up by opening the folder so the attached pieces are in a vertical row with the picture fastened upside down to the top section, the window in the middle, and the plain section at the bottom. Fold the bottom piece up upon the window and the top piece down on that and have it folded that way on your table.

Start by showing the front and back of the closed folder, with no picture in the window. Hold the window facing front. With your right hand, lift the back piece straight up to the top and shake the folder open so the bottom part falls down and the whole thing hangs down from your right hand in a vertical row.

The audience can look right through the open window and the entire frame seems to be empty. Keep it that way, hanging down from your right hand. Bring your left palm against the *front* of the window and tilt the window back and up until it rests flatly on your left palm. The opening of the window is now toward the floor.

THE GHOST FRAME

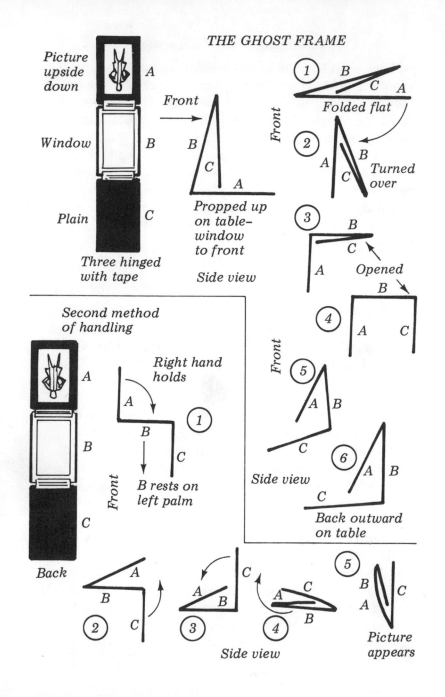

Picture upside down — A

Window — B

Plain — C

Three hinged with tape

Front →

Side view

B

C

A

Propped up on table— window to front

① Folded flat
B
C A

② Turned over
A
C B

③ Opened
B
C
A

④ B
A C

⑤ Side view
A B
C

⑥ Back outward on table
A B
C

Second method of handling

A

B

C

Back

① Right hand holds
A
B
C
B rests on left palm

Front

② A
B
C

③ Side view
A
B
C

④ A C
B

⑤ Picture appears
B C
A

With your right hand, fold the top piece down upon the window, which secretly brings the picture into position. Then fold the bottom piece up over the top piece. Keep the closed folder, window down, on the palm of your left hand. Snap your right finger and thumb. Lift up the frame and show that the picture has appeared in the window.

Here are some examples of tricks you can do with the frame:

A Work of Art

"May I show you a valuable work of art?" you ask as you call attention to the empty frame. You glance at it yourself, shake your head, and apologize. "Oh, I'm sorry. It's still invisible, isn't it? I usually keep it that way because there have been so many thefts of valuable paintings and engravings. If any thief saw this, he would think there was no picture in it at all."

You show both sides of the frame and prop it up back outward on your table again or hold it face down on your hand. "But you all look like honest people. I'm sure I can trust you . . . and I do want you to see this, so I'll make it visible for you. It's a very excellent engraving of our first President, George Washington."

As you turn the frame around, the audience can see that a folded dollar bill has appeared. You remove the bill, unfold it and show it, and then put it away in your pocket as you smile and say, "Believe me, this is a work of art that is really worth money."

To set it up fold both ends of a dollar bill so the engraving of Washington shows at the front of it. Have it attached to the top section of the frame with four snapshot corner mounts so you can remove it easily to unfold it and show the audience that it is a dollar bill.

The Invisible Mirror

"Do you remember the story of Snow White and the magic mirror?" you ask. " 'Mirror, mirror on the wall, who's the fairest of them all?' " You show the empty frame. "This is a magic mirror—an invisible mirror. To most people it would seem that there is no mirror there at all. But you can still look into it and see the truth reflected."

You show the empty frame front and back and turn it so the window is toward you. Pretending to admire yourself in the invisible mirror, you say, "I thought at first that this was a picture of a great magician." Slowly you turn the frame around. In what was the empty window, there is now a silvery mirror. You hold it facing the audience, tilting it as if to catch their reflections in it and say, "But the truth is that it really reflects . . . one of the nicest audiences in the world."

For this you need a 4″ by 6″ sheet of shiny aluminum foil. Make sure it is free of wrinkles and attach it smoothly to the top section of the frame, with strips of cloth tape along its edges or with double-stick tape at the back. Because the "mirror" will cover almost the entire section and there is no margin left at the bottom for propping the frame open on your table at the start, the second method of handling it, by keeping it in your hand, should be used.

Signed Card in Frame

Someone chooses a card from the pack and writes his signature across the face of it while you turn your head away so you can't see which card he chose. He returns it to the pack so it is lost among the others and you put the pack aside.

You show an empty picture frame and ask him to focus

his thoughts upon it while you attempt to read his mind and tell him which card was his. After a few tries, you announce the name of the card and then explain that you were able to read his thoughts because he projected such a clear mental picture. When you show him the front of the frame again, his chosen card has appeared in it, and you take the frame to him so he can identify his signature on the card.

Set it up by attaching a short strip of double-stick tape to the center of the top section of the frame folder. Fold it so that section becomes the base and have the empty frame propped up, window outward, on your table. You will also need a pen and a pack of cards that includes The Long One, the trick card with the taped edge that was explained in Chapter 1.

Have a card chosen, hand the person the pen, and ask him to write his signature boldly across the face of the card while you turn your head so you can't see which one he took. Have him turn the card face down and return it to the pack. Cut the pack a few times so his card apparently is lost among the others and use The Long One to bring it to the top.

"I'll put the pack aside," you say as you return to your table, "and ask you just to think of your card while I attempt to read your mind." Actually you put the pack aside by resting it *face up* right on top of the strip of double-stick tape attached to the frame. Press down a little so that the top card of the pack, the one he signed, will stick to the tape. Leave the pack there on the table behind the frame and walk a few steps away.

Pretend to try to read his mind, then admit that the "mental picture isn't clear," and say, "Maybe this will help . . ." Turn back to the table, pick up the pack of cards, and casually put it to one side, secretly leaving the chosen card attached to the hidden base of the frame. "It's a picture frame . . . without any picture," you explain. "Please focus your thoughts upon it as if you were gazing into a crystal ball and let's see if I can capture an imaginary picture of the card you have in mind."

Take up the frame, show it front and back so that it is seen empty, and prop it up on the table again with its back to the audience. Look at the card that is now framed in it so that only you can see it, then look at the person and say, "The picture is becoming clearer. I see a red card, a Diamond—the Five of Diamonds [or whatever it is]. Was that your card?"

When he acknowledges that you were right, you say, "I was able to read your thoughts because you projected a very clear mental picture—so clear I could almost see the card itself." Slowly you turn the frame around and reveal the card in it. "As a matter of fact, it is the exact card you chose. It even has your name on it." Pick up the frame, carry it to him, and have him identify it. "That is your signature, isn't it?"

DOUBLE DOUBLE FOLDER

This folder looks like two flat pieces of cardboard hinged at the center so it can be opened wide to show it inside and out. It can be used for the vanish, appearance, or change of handkerchiefs, loops of ribbon, and many other things that allow for creating unusual magical effects. Almost anything that will fit flatly into one of its secret sides can be changed for anything else hidden in a second side.

What you need:
Four pieces of poster board in any desired color, each 7" by 11".
Cloth adhesive tape in a contrasting color, ¾" wide.
A pencil, scissors, and a ruler.

How you make it:

Put one of the pieces of poster board on a table, narrow ends top and bottom. Take a 7″ length of cloth tape and attach half its width across the top edge of the board and then bend the tape down over that edge to fasten it across the back, thus binding the top edge with a border of tape. Bind the top edge of a second piece of the poster board the same way.

Place one piece on top of the other so all the edges exactly meet and fasten their side edges together at both sides with 11″ lengths of tape, again by attaching half the width of the tape to the top surface and bending it over to fasten it at the rear. You now have two pieces bound together at the sides, bound separately at the top so there is an opening between them, and with no tape across the bottom edges.

For a moment, put those two aside. Take the other two pieces and prepare them the same way, binding each of their top edges separately with tape and then putting one board on top of the other and binding both side edges of the two together.

Place both double pieces vertically on the table so the untaped end of one touches the untaped end of the other. Separate them about ⅛″ and hinge the two together by binding them where they almost meet with a 9″ length of tape. Bend the extra ends of that tape around the sides to the rear. Turn the whole thing over and reinforce the hinge by attaching another strip across where the pieces are joined.

You should have what looks like two flat pieces of cardboard hinged together at the center and bound around all the edges with tape. But since each side really is double there are two secret sections. If you close the folder there are three openings at the top: into the secret front section, into the center of the folder itself, and into the secret rear section.

The set-up:

To try the handling, close the folder so the three openings are at the top. Tuck a small blue handkerchief down into the front secret section to hide it there and a small yellow handkerchief into the secret section at the rear.

How you use it:

Pick up the folder with your left hand at the top, fingers in front and thumb at the rear. Hold it closed with the flat front surface toward the audience. Bring your right hand to it with the back of that hand toward the audience and so that your thumb will slide down into the top of the folder.

Hold the top of the front section between your right thumb and fingers and the top of the rear section between your left thumb and fingers. Move your right hand out and down to open out the folder and show the inside to the audience. In opening it, your right thumb and finger should keep what is now the bottom end pinched shut so that whatever is hidden in that section will not drop out.

With both hands still in that position, left hand at the top and right hand at the bottom, turn the opened folder around to show the back of it to the audience. Then turn it the way it was and close it again by folding the bottom part up against the top. You have now shown it empty inside and front and back.

Hold it by the top with your left hand. Slide your right-hand fingers into the rear section and pull out the yellow handkerchief. To the audience it looks as though you are producing it from the center part of the folder that you just showed empty.

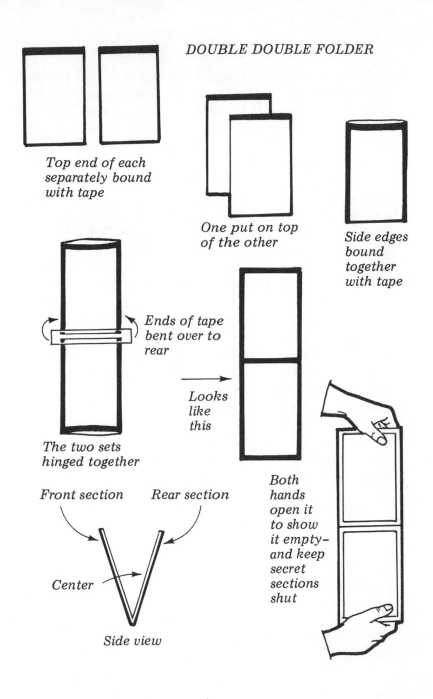

DOUBLE DOUBLE FOLDER

Top end of each separately bound with tape

One put on top of the other

Side edges bound together with tape

Ends of tape bent over to rear

The two sets hinged together

Looks like this

Front section

Rear section

Center

Side view

Both hands open it to show it empty—and keep secret sections shut

Display the yellow handkerchief and then tuck it back down inside the rear section so it is hidden there again. Open out the folder to show the center as before, and the yellow handkerchief seems to have disappeared. Close it up and with your right hand take out the yellow handkerchief again. It has reappeared.

Tuck it back into the rear section once more. Snap your fingers and reach into the front section and draw out the other handkerchief. Display it and open out the folder to show that it is otherwise empty. The yellow handkerchief, after appearing, vanishing, and reappearing, has changed to blue.

Both ends of the folder should always be held when it is opened or closed. Whenever you put anything into the top or take anything from it the illusion should be that you are reaching down into the center, not into the side sections.

The sides may bulge slightly when things are hidden in them, but that is nothing to be concerned about since the audience is given only a brief look at the opened folder each time, and any slight bending of the flexible cardboard in handling it seems natural. Things that are extremely bulky should not be used, but the two sections are quite roomy.

Here are some tricks that suggest various ways the folder can be used:

Sock Ending

You repeatedly vanish a handkerchief and try to make it reappear. But each time it appears it changes color. Finally the trick turns out right—and then the handkerchief turns into a sock.

For this you will need three handkerchiefs—yellow, blue and green—and a man's sock, preferably black and of fairly thin material.

Fold the sock in half and slide it flatly into the bottom of the folder's front section. Put first the yellow and then the blue handkerchief into that section with the sock. Hide the green handkerchief in the rear section.

"I'd like to show you something new that I've been working on. It's a simple little trick with a cardboard folder," you say as you open out the folder, show it empty, and close it again. "I count one-two-three . . . and a green handkerchief appears."

Reach into the rear section, take out the green handkerchief, show it, and then tuck it back inside the rear section again. "I count three-two-one . . . and it disappears." Open the folder to show that it has vanished and close it. "One-two-three . . . and the green handkerchief appears once more . . ." Reach into the front section and instead of taking out the green handkerchief pull out the blue one, but don't look at it directly for a moment. Then glance at it, appear surprised, shake your head and say, "Let me try it again. This is a little trick . . . with a blue handkerchief . . ."

Push the blue one down into the rear section to hide it. Count aloud, "Three-two-one." Open the folder to show that it has disappeared. Close the folder and say, "One-two-three . . . and the little blue handkerchief appears . . ." Reach into the front section and pull out the yellow one instead of the blue one. Stare at it a moment and say, "What's happening here? The trick worked when I did it at home. Let's try just once more. This is a little trick with a—yellow handkerchief . . ." Tuck the yellow one into the rear section. "Three-two-one." Open the folder, show that it has disappeared, close the folder and say, "One-two-three . . . and the little yellow handkerchief appears . . ."

Hesitate a moment. Close your eyes and reach into the rear section and pull out the yellow handkerchief slowly.

Open your eyes, look at it, and smile broadly when you see that it *is* yellow. "Thank goodness. I've got it now . . . I think I'd better quit while I'm ahead."

Put the yellow one into the rear section. "The only part I haven't worked out is some way to end this trick. I wish I had a real *sock* ending." Reach into the folder and pull out the sock and say, "There—how's that?" Open the folder to show it otherwise empty, close it up, and put it aside.

Vanishing and Linking Ribbon Loops

Three loops of colored ribbon vanish one at a time and then reappear linked together.

You will need six ribbons, each about 1″ wide and 2′ long: two red, two white, and two blue. Tie the two ends of one of the red ones, thread a white one through that and knot its ends, and tie a blue one through the white so you have a chain of three loops. Fold them flat and slide them into the front section of the folder. Tie each of the other ribbons into a separate loop and have them with the folder on your table.

Pick up the three separate loops one at a time, show them, and put your right hand through them so they hang over that arm and leave your hand free. Take the folder with both hands, open it out and show both sides, and close it up again. Hold the folder with your left hand and with the fingers of that hand draw one of the loops off your right arm and then transfer the loop to your right hand. With your right hand, tuck it down into the rear section of the folder. Snap your fingers, take the folder with both hands, open it and show that the ribbon has disappeared.

Vanish the second and third loops the same way. Then reach into the front section and slowly pull out the three loops linked together into a chain. Display them, gather them up, and open the folder once more to show that it is empty.

Just One Wish

Take a necktie and fold it back and forth upon itself in accordion pleats about 6" long. Slide it flatly into the rear section of the folder. Put a birthday greeting card into the center section. Tie a bright ribbon around the outside of the folder so that it somewhat resembles a gift package. The ribbon should be tied off with a bow knot so you can untie it quickly just by pulling one end.

"Will you excuse me while I open this?" you ask, as you show the folder wrapped as a gift package. "It's a birthday gift from a magician friend of mine." Pull open the bow knot, remove the ribbon, and drop it to your table.

Hold the folder upright with your left hand and spread it far enough apart at the top so your right hand can reach into the side and remove the birthday card from the center section. Take out the card, glance at it, and put it on the table. Then open the folder wide with both hands to show it empty, close it again, and keep it held with your left hand at the top.

"Just a birthday card," you say as you pick up the card with your right hand and pretend to read from it: " 'Happy birthday. You are entitled to one magic wish—but just one. Anything you wish for shall be yours . . .' "

Shake your head and toss the card back on the table. "How do you like that guy? A magic wish. Even if he is a magician, he doesn't think I believe that, does he? I mean . . . he could have sent me *something*. At least he could have sent me a necktie. I really wish he—"

Jerk the folder in your left hand suddenly and break off

your words. Turn your head slowly and stare at the folder. "You don't think . . . Oh, no . . . It couldn't be!" Reach into the folder and slowly pull out the necktie. Throw the folder on the table and stare at the necktie. "Just one wish. I could have wished for a million dollars. But I had to wish for a necktie!" Sigh heavily and shake your head as you drop the tie to the table and then say, "Oh, well . . . maybe next year."

TILT A TRAY

Tilt this small tray to one side and it adds a number of cards, coins, or other things to those that were dropped into it. Tip it the other direction and it secretly takes some away. Because the same tray either adds or takes away, according to which direction you tip it as you pour things from it, it serves a double purpose as a utility device.

What you need:
Two identical small cardboard food-carrier trays, the kind used by markets for the packaging and display of fresh fruits, meats, and vegetables. Both must be the same size and color and have flat bottoms with no ridges or separations. They should be about 4″ wide, 8″ long, and 1″ deep.
Black cloth adhesive tape, 1⅛″ wide.
A pack of cards, to help adjust the height of the device that is to be built into the tray.
A pencil, scissors, and a ruler.

How you make it:
Turn one of the matching trays upside down. Measure half the length of it and draw a vertical line across the center. Cut the tray vertically in half so you have two

separate pieces. Take one of the half-trays and trim off its top rim.

Deal fifteen cards off the pack and square them up. Turn the full tray, the one that is not cut, lengthwise. Stack the squared packet of cards lengthwise in the bottom of it against its left end. Put the half-tray down on top of the cards inside the uncut tray. Because of the stack of cards, there is a space of about ¼" between the two bottoms. The outer sides of the half-tray should fit against the inner sides of the whole tray. You may have to trim a little more off the top of the half-tray so it fits down inside.

When you have the half-tray positioned properly, fasten it into place with three strips of tape, one over the double rim at the left end, the others over the double rims at each side. Tilt the tray to the right, shake out the cards, and put them aside. Bind the cut front edge of the half-tray across from rim to rim by fastening half the width of a strip of tape to it and bending the tape up under the edge. Work your little finger in under it to fasten the tape smoothly to the underside.

The final step is to trim the entire top rim of the tray with a tape binding that matches the center strip. Start by attaching a short strip lengthwise near one end of the outside of the tray just beneath the outer rim and bend it over the top of the rim to the inside. Then fasten another lengthwise strip, matching it evenly, bending it over to the inside and attaching it the same way, and so on, all the way around the top edge of the tray.

You should now have a tray with what amounts to a shelf at the left half, with a space between it and the bottom of the rest of the tray itself. A card or coin dropped into the bottom at the right side will slide under the shelf when the tray is tipped to the left. If the tray is tipped to the right, it will slide out from under the shelf again.

TILT A TRAY

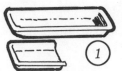

Cardboard food tray and half of another (1)

Half tray taped inside end of whole one (2)

(3) **Side view**

(4) **Cut edge of half-tray bound with tape**

(5) **All outer and inner edges bound with tape**

Two coins dropped on shelf. Three coins dropped into bottom

Trap tipped left only two pour into hand

Tray tipped right all five pour into hand

Ten cards counted into tray

Eight cards on shelf

Two cards in bottom of tray

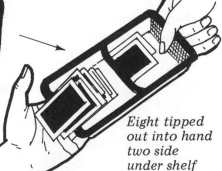

Eight tipped out into hand two side under shelf

The set-up:
To try it, put the tray lengthwise on your table, the shelf part to the left. Have five coins, all the same denomination, on the table beside it.

How you use it:
Stand behind the table. Pick up one of the coins with your right hand, hold it a few inches above the tray, and drop it so that it falls to the bottom at the right side. Aloud, count, "One." Count a second coin and then a third one as you drop them into that side of the tray. Move your hand a little to the left, and with no break in the counting, drop a fourth coin and a fifth so those two fall into the tray on top of the shelf.

Cup your left palm upward in front of you. With your right hand, pick up the tray at its right-hand end. Tilt the tray to the left and toward you to pour the coins into your cupped left hand. Close those fingers around them. Put the tray back on the table, right side up as before.

You have openly counted five coins and poured them into your hand. Now hold your closed left hand above the tray. Drop first one coin and then the second one into the tray, counting them aloud. Open your hand and show that three of the coins have vanished.

With your left hand, take the tray at its left end and tip it toward you to the right to pour the coins into your cupped right hand. This time those that were under the shelf pour into your hand with the others. Put the tray back on the table. Drop the coins one at a time into the tray from your right hand as you count them. Magically you have five again.

Handling It with Cards

Now try the tray with cards. Deal two cards, one at a time, so they drop lengthwise into the right side of the tray. Count them aloud, and without breaking the rhythm, count eight more cards into the left side, on top of the shelf. Put the pack aside.

With your right hand, pick up the tray at its right end, tilt it to the left and over toward you and tip the cards out into your left hand. Put the tray back on the table. You have counted ten, one at a time, into the tray. But only eight tip out into your hand because the other two slide under the shelf.

Square them and place that packet to one side of your table. Take the pack again and deal eight cards lengthwise into the left side of the tray on top of the shelf as you count them aloud. Put aside the pack. With your left hand, pick up the tray at its left end, tilt it over toward you to the right and tip the cards into your right hand. As you tip it, the two cards that were under the shelf will slide out with the others. Put back the tray, square that packet of cards, and place them at the other side of the table.

Pretend to make two cards invisibly fly from one packet to the other. Count the first packet and show that two are missing. Then count the second pile and show that you have ten instead of only eight.

The Cards Across

This is a more elaborate version of the invisible flight of two cards from one packet to another, using the tray and the same method of handling. Ten cards are counted out and two of them are freely chosen by members of the audience before the cards are dropped into a plastic bag.

Ten more cards are counted and put into a second plastic bag. Magically the two chosen cards pass from one plastic bag to the other.

You will need two packs of cards with matching backs, two plastic sandwich bags, and the tray. To set it up, take one of the packs, deal off ten cards and discard them to reduce the size of the pack. Deal eight more cards face up in a row on the table. Look through the second pack, remove the duplicates of those eight cards, and put the second pack aside. Stack the eight duplicates together and put them on top of the remainder of the first pack. Gather the eight face-up cards and put those face down on top of the duplicates. Then put two more cards on top of those.

From the top down, the pack is now stacked so that you have two indifferent cards, then a set of eight, then eight duplicates of that set. Put the pack face down in the tray and have it on your table with the two plastic bags beside it.

Pick up the pack and deal ten cards, one at a time, counting them as you put the first two to the right side of the tray and the rest on top of the shelf to the left. Put the pack aside. Tilt the tray to the left and toward you and tip the cards into your left hand. Continue to tip the tray over until it is upside down, to indicate that there are no other cards in it, and then turn it upright and put it back on the table.

"Ten cards," you say, although you really have only eight because two remain hidden under the shelf of the tray. Hold the packet high with your left hand. Take one of the plastic sandwich bags with your other hand, show it, and tuck it temporarily into the top of your breast pocket.

Go to someone in the audience. Have him freely select one of the cards and ask him to show it to those around him without letting you see it. Let him keep the card for a moment as you go to a second person and have another card chosen. Hand the second person the rest of the cards and ask him to put his card back among them and to shuffle them.

"I don't want to touch those cards again," you say as you take the plastic bag from your breast pocket and open it. "Now that you've mixed them so that your card is lost among them, will you please drop them all into this bag?" When he has done that, carry the bag back to the first person and say, "Will you put your card down somewhere in the center of these?"

Hold the bag above your head and return to your table. Fold the bag and toss it to the floor at the left. Show your hands empty, pick up the pack and count out ten more cards, dealing them one at a time into the tray on top of the shelf. Put the pack aside. Tilt the tray toward you and to the right, tip the cards into your right hand, and put the tray back on the table. Take the other plastic bag, drop those cards into it, fold the bag and toss it to the floor at your right.

"Now, if I could find the two chosen cards and make them invisible," you say, "it would be a simple matter to carry them from one bag to the other so you couldn't see me do it." Walk over to the bag on the floor at the left, tap your foot on it, bend your foot up and pretend to pluck an invisible card from the sole of your shoe. Walk across to the bag on the floor at your right and pretend to drop the invisible card down into that bag.

"There's one." Go back to the first bag. "That leaves nine here and puts eleven over there. This time, I'll do it the hard way. I'll throw the card across." Bend down, pick up the bag, pretend to draw a second invisible card from it, and toss it toward the bag on the floor at the right. Shake the bag in your hand. "If the magic has worked, there should be only eight cards left."

Take them from the bag. Count them off, one at a time, dropping the cards singly to the floor. "Eight there are." Crush the bag, drop it, and brush your hands together. Walk over, pick up the other bag, take out the cards, toss the empty bag aside and slowly count those cards, *backs outward,* from hand to hand, "Exactly twelve—which means the two chosen cards must be among them."

Turn to the first person who selected one, ask him to call out the name of it, look through the cards for the duplicate and hold it up to show it. Then ask the second person to name his card and show that.

Secretly Adding Cards to a Shuffled Pack

The tray provides a simple means of adding trick cards to an ordinary pack or adding a prearranged stack of cards to the top or bottom of a pack shuffled by someone in the audience.

For example, say that you want to add four Aces to the top of the pack. Set it up by previously stacking the four Aces face up, sliding them under the tray's shelf, and resting the pack face up on top of the shelf.

Pick up the tray at its right end and tilt it toward you to the left to tip the pack into your left hand. Have someone shuffle the cards and then take the pack and casually rest it face up on the shelf of the tray again, to free your hands to pick up something else, or while you talk for a moment.

When you are ready to use the pack again, pick up the tray at its left end and tilt it enough to the right so the pack slides from the shelf to the bottom. The stacked cards will slide from under the shelf so they are added to the pack. Then continue to tilt the tray over and tip the pack into your right hand. Put the tray back on the table. You have the four Aces on top of the pack.

Using the Tray As a Switching Device

If you are performing on a platform or far enough from a seated audience so the tray on your table is above the eye level of those watching, it can be used to switch sets of cards, coins, poker chips, or such things as round metal-rimmed tags that bear colors or designs.

Say that you wish to force someone to choose the color red. Print or crayon five metal-rimmed tags each a different color, including red, and five more that are all red. Have the five red ones on the shelf of the tray and those of various colors stacked on the table beside the tray.

Explain to the audience that you have a number of tags of various colors. Pick one up, call the color aloud, show both sides, and drop it into the bottom of the tray to the right. Continue until you have shown all the tags. Pick up the tray at the right end, tip it over toward you to the left, pour the tags into your cupped hand, and put back the tray with your other hand. The tags of different colors all slide under the shelf so that those in your left hand are now all red. Keep that hand closed around them.

Go to someone in the audience, hold both hands cupped together, and ask the person to shut his eyes and reach into your hands and take any tag he wishes. As soon as he has taken one, casually drop the rest of the tags into your jacket pocket and leave them there. He has, of course, "chosen" red.

THE DISSOLVING DIE

A large black die with white spots is dropped into an empty tube. When you lift the tube, the die has vanished and in its place is a glass of white liquid. You push your hand right through the tube and fold it flat to prove the die has disappeared completely. As you pour the white liquid from the glass, you explain, "There's nothing left of it but its spots—and even those have melted."

What you need:
White poster board.
Black self-adhesive decorative paper.
Black cloth adhesive tape, ¾" wide.
White round ¾" self-sticking labels, available in stationery stores for use as price stickers.
Two rather squat, broad-mouthed glasses, about 3¼" high and 3" in diameter at the top.
Enough milk to fill one of the glasses.
A pencil, scissors, and a ruler.

How you make it:
The "die" is a hollow square box with no bottom and a top that hinges open like a lid. It folds flat inside the tube when the tube is folded flat.

Measure and cut five pieces of cardboard each 3½" square. Place four of them side by side in a horizontal row on a table so there is a space of about ¹⁄₁₆" between them. Fasten them together with vertical strips of cloth tape. Stand the attached pieces upright, form them into a square, and tape the two remaining edges together at the inside.

Turn the square on one side so there is an open part to the right. Tape the fifth piece of cardboard to the bottom edge of that, again allowing enough space for the tape to act as a hinge.

You should have what amounts to a bottomless square box with a hinged lid that lies flat on top. If you squeeze its diagonal corners together, the whole thing will fold flat.

The outside should be covered with the black self-adhesive paper. Cut the paper into 4" squares to allow enough for overlapping at the sides and to fold it over the edges to the inside at the top and bottom. The small round labels serve as die spots and should be fastened into place in the usual die pattern, with a six-spot at the front, five-spot on top, four-spot one side, three-spot the other side, and a one-spot at the rear.

To make the tube that is used to cover the die, cut four pieces of cardboard each 4″ by 8″. With vertical strips of the black cloth tape, hinge the four together into a tube, with enough space between the pieces so the tube may be folded flat. The result should be a tube 8″ high by 4″ wide, open at the top and bottom so the die will easily drop through it. For decoration, fasten horizontal bands of black tape around the top and bottom edges of the tube.

The set-up:

Fill one of the glasses with milk and put that at the left front side of your table as you stand behind it. Cover the glass with the tube so the audience will not know the glass is there. Place the squared-up die beside the tube to the right, with the hinged side of its lid toward the front. The other empty glass should be out of the way at the rear of the table.

How you use it:

Bring your right hand down over the die and grasp it between your thumb at the left side near the top and your fingers at the right side so as to hold its square shape. Lift it a little, tilt it slightly forward to make it less likely that anyone in front will see the hollow bottom, and tap the bottom front edge of it on the table once or twice as if to prove that the die is solid.

Keep it tilted slightly forward, bring it up, and drop it down inside the tube from the top. With your left hand, lift

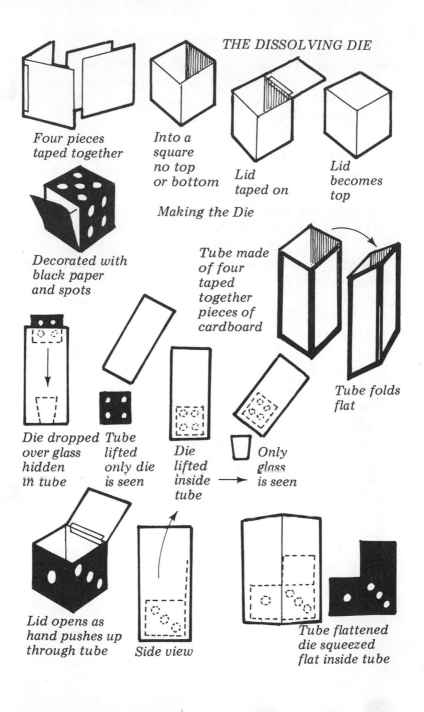

THE DISSOLVING DIE

Four pieces taped together

Into a square no top or bottom

Lid taped on

Lid becomes top

Making the Die

Decorated with black paper and spots

Tube made of four taped together pieces of cardboard

Tube folds flat

Die dropped over glass hidden in tube

Tube lifted only die is seen

Die lifted inside tube

Only glass is seen

Lid opens as hand pushes up through tube

Side view

Tube flattened die squeezed flat inside tube

the tube straight up off the die, which now covers the glass of milk so it is hidden. It should look as though you just dropped the die through the tube as proof that there is nothing in the tube.

Hold up the tube with both hands so the audience can look through it. Push your right arm and hand up through the tube from the bottom, wave your fingers as they come out the top, withdraw your arm, and then put the tube down over the die on the table.

Take the bottom of the tube with your left hand, thumb at the rear and fingers in front. Squeeze the tube slightly to hold the die hidden inside it and lift the tube straight up, lifting the hidden die with it, to reveal the glass of milk on the table.

While your left hand continues to hold the tube and hidden die, bring your right hand under the tube. Push that hand and arm up through the tube again, lifting the lid of the hidden die automatically as your hand goes up through the tube. The lid opens upward against the inside of the tube which conceals it. Wave your fingers as they show at the top.

Withdraw your right arm and hand completely from the tube, and as you do, squeeze the tube flat with your left hand. The die, still hidden inside, flattens with the tube. Keep a tight grip with your left hand, turn the flat tube to the right so its side edge is toward the audience, and leave the tube at the rear of the table.

All of this should take only a moment as you show that the die has vanished and put the tube aside. Pick up the glass of milk with your left hand, take the empty glass with your right hand, and pour "the white liquid spots of the die" from glass to glass.

Other Ways to Use It

Instead of changing the die to a glass of milk, you can change it into an orange, an apple, a stack of gold coins, or a pack of cards standing on end in a card case. You can use any small object that will fit under the hollow die and tie it in with whatever magical plot you want to build around it.

You can also "shrink" the large die into a small one. For that, make a smaller die of a child's alphabet block by covering it with black adhesive paper and decorating it with white spots. Have it hidden under the tube at the start as the glass of milk was. Then drop the large die into the tube and lift the tube to reveal the small one as you show that the big die has vanished.

THE GOLDFISH TRIANGLE

A triangular screen stands on your table. You open out its three panels and show both sides of them, one side red and the other side blue, and then form them into a triangle again. When you lift it from the table, a bowl of water and goldfish appear.

What you need:
Four 9" by 12" pieces of red poster board and four 9" by 12" pieces of blue poster board.

Black cloth adhesive tape, 1½" wide.

A clamp-type clothespin.

A small, upright flat-sided clear glass goldfish bowl that will fit within the screen when it is folded into a triangle. It should be about 5" high and 4½" square at its base. A good substitute is a large apothecary jar with a round mouth and square sides, such as those sold in many variety stores and gift shops, without its lid.

Water and goldfish, or a few pieces of raw carrot cut to somewhat resemble goldfish.

A pair of scissors.

How you make it:

Put one of the red pieces of poster board squarely on top of one of the blue pieces, narrow ends top and bottom, and bind their top and bottom edges together with lengthwise strips of the black cloth tape by fastening half its width to one side and turning it over the edge to fasten it to the other side. Bind the remaining pieces of poster board together the same way to give you four panels that are red one side and blue the other side.

Put two of them side by side on a table with their red sides up, separate them a little more than ¼″, and hinge them together with a vertical strip of the cloth tape, joining both pieces from top to bottom. Hinge a third panel, red side up, to the side of the second and a fourth to the side of the third, allowing space between each of them, so that you have a horizontal row of four attached panels.

Turn the whole thing over and attach matching vertical lengths of tape at the back to reinforce each of the hinges. Then bind the side edges of the two outer panels at the left and right of the row of four. Fold the screen back and forth on itself to flex the hinges so all the panels will fold easily in any direction.

The set-up:

Although the screen has four panels, it is positioned and handled so the audience believes there are only three and that the red and blue sides of those three are shown. The bowl of goldfish remains hidden behind one of the panels at all times. That panel is never moved from its original position and the audience never sees the rear side of it.

To set it in position, first put the partly filled bowl of water and goldfish, or imitation fish, at the center of the table you will use when performing. Open out the screen so the four panels are upright in a horizontal row. Take the fourth panel, the one at the far right, and close it in toward you and around behind until it is folded flat against the back of the third panel.

Rest the bottom edge of that upright double panel on the table directly in front of the fishbowl so the bowl is hidden behind it from the view of the audience. In all the handling that follows, that panel is never lifted from the table or moved left or right. It must be kept resting on its bottom edge in front of the bowl, upright and held squarely toward the audience.

Hold that panel where it is and turn the other two panels back around the bowl, bringing the one at the extreme left back and around to the right to form a triangle around the bowl. Clamp the top corners of the two panels at the right together with the clothespin to hold the triangle in place.

How you use it:

What you are about to do is open out the screen and without lifting it from the table aparently show one side of the three panels, fold them together, show the other side of the three, and then form it into a triangle again. Stand to the right of the table. Remove the clothespin and keep it in your right hand, but so the thumb and first two fingers of that hand are free.

With that right hand, grasp the top edge of the front double panel at its center, thumb at the rear and two fingers in front. Hold that panel as it is, with its front squarely toward the audience. With your left hand, grasp the panel nearest to you and turn it all the way out to the left, opening the screen until the three panels are held in a horizontal

THE GOLDFISH TRIANGLE

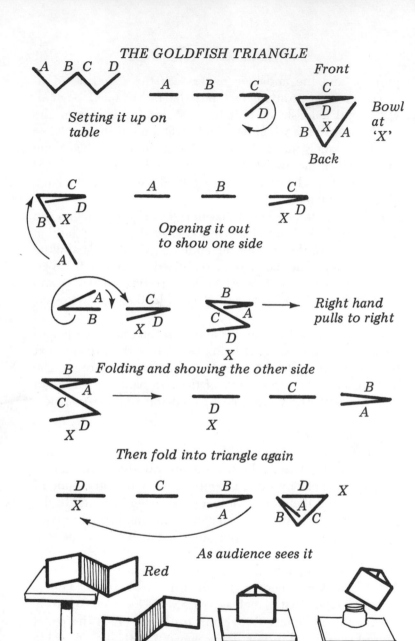

Setting it up on table

Front

Bowl at 'X'

Back

Opening it out to show one side

Right hand pulls to right

Folding and showing the other side

Then fold into triangle again

As audience sees it

Red

Blue

row. The three panels are now in a straight line, their fronts toward the audience. You have apparently shown one side of the screen.

Close the panel at the far left of the row, *outward* from left to right to fold the face of it against the face of the next panel as if you were closing a book. Then fold both of those together from left to right against the face of the third panel. The screen has now been folded so all the upright panels stand flatly together.

Keep the folded screen held upright with your left hand. Move your right hand over to grasp the two front panels *together* at the center of the right edge. With your left hand, grasp the top of the *single* panel that is at the rear of the folded screen, directly in front of the fishbowl, and hold that where it is. Draw your right hand straight out to the right, unfolding the screen so all three panels are in a horizontal row. You have now apparently shown the other side of the screen.

Bring your right hand to the rear and around to form the panels into a triangle again. Clamp its open corners together with the clothespin. Snap your fingers, clap your hands, or wave a wand. Then just lift the triangle straight up off the table and show the fishbowl that has appeared.

In print, the handling may seem complicated, but it is really a simple matter of unfolding the screen to one side of the stationary center panel and then to the other side, as you will discover if you follow the moves slowly a few times with the screen in hand. When performing, it should all be done rather rapidly.

Unusual Things to Produce

Instead of a fishbowl, you might produce a small solid statue, a battery-lighted lantern, a vase with real flowers that could be given to members of the audience, a book, a sports trophy, a football, a shoe, or something else that fits whatever story you want to build around the trick. With a slightly larger screen, made and handled the same way, you could produce a stack of several bricks, or even a heavy bowling ball.

4

BOXES, CARTONS,
AND TUBES

THE MATCHLESS MATCHBOX

You show a large kitchen matchbox empty and then slide
the drawer back inside the cover. A moment later you open
the box again, remove the drawer completely from the
cover, and it is now filled with silk handkerchiefs, dollar
bills, a pack of playing cards, or whatever else you want to
produce. Since the drawer itself is free of trickery, it may
even be handed to someone in the audience so he can
remove the things from it.

What you need:
   Two large empty identical kitchen cardboard matchboxes
of standard size, approximately 2½″ wide, slightly less than
5″ long, and about 1½″ deep. These are the type with a
drawer that slides into the cover. You want the plain ones,
not boxes with fancy decorated covers but the kind clearly
labeled "Kitchen Safety Matches," so the audience will
immediately recognize the box as a common object used in
most homes.

A ruler, pencil, and a pair of scissors.
Whatever you intend to produce from the box.

How you make it:

Because such matchboxes are manufactured of fairly thin
and flexible cardboard, the cover of one will accommodate
not only its own drawer but also part of a drawer from
another box, fitted under it so both slide inside the cover
together. It is this dummy drawer that is first shown empty
and then left hidden inside the cover when the real drawer
is removed at the end of the trick. Together they fit rather
tightly into the cover, which helps in handling the box.

Take the drawer from one of the boxes, discard that
cover, and turn the empty drawer mouth downward on a
table. Lay the ruler on the upturned bottom, measure in ⅜"
from one end, and make a pencil mark across the bottom
and down both sides. Cut that end off the box by cutting up
one side, across the bottom and down the other side, and
throw away the cut-off piece.

The remainder will be the dummy drawer. Turn it mouth
upward, measure in about ½" from the cut end, and draw a
bold pencil line down both sides. That mark is made so that
when you later pull the dummy drawer out of the cover you
can see just how far to pull it and stop at that mark.

Now take the whole drawer from the second matchbox
and slide that *inside* the cut end of the dummy drawer. Push
it all the way into the dummy drawer so the two are nested
and slide them together into the matchbox cover.

The set-up:

To try the handling, put a handkerchief, crumpled tissue,
or some small object into the real drawer. Close the box and
turn it lengthwise with its double end toward the right.
Push in the end at the left so both drawers come part way

out of the cover at the right. Separate those two ends until you can put your finger down between them. Then push the whole drawer back into the cover until its right end is flush with that end of the cover. Leave about ½″ of the dummy drawer sticking out of the cover to the right.

How you use it:

Stand behind the table, turn your left hand palm down and bring it over the box. Pick it up with your thumb against the side toward you and your second, third, and little fingers against the far side. Rest your first finger at the right end of the cover so the tip of that finger goes down inside between the end of the cover and the open end of the dummy drawer.

Still holding it with your left hand, turn the box so that end is toward the audience. Grip the top of the open end of the dummy drawer with your right thumb and first finger and pull it out, pressing back with the tip of your left finger to keep the real drawer from sliding out with it. Glance down at the side of the box so as not to open the dummy drawer beyond the pencil line marked at the side.

Take your right hand away and tilt the box down so the front end is toward the floor and the audience can look into the box. To those looking inside, the front end of the real drawer appears to be the inside rear end of the dummy drawer. You can now handle the box freely with either hand to show it. Transfer it to your right hand so you can show the open drawer to those seated at that side.

When you have finished showing it empty, take it with your left hand so the palm of that hand is against the back end of the cover. Turn the box lengthwise and shut it by pushing the dummy drawer in with your right hand. Drop the closed box on the table *with the double end toward the rear* and leave it there a moment.

THE MATCHLESS MATCHBOX

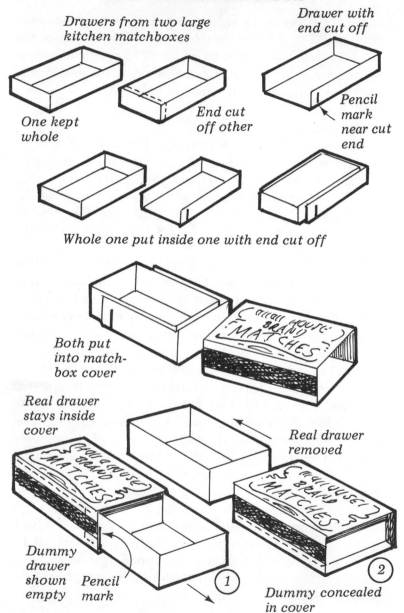

Drawers from two large kitchen matchboxes

Drawer with end cut off

One kept whole

End cut off other

Pencil mark near cut end

Whole one put inside one with end cut off

Both put into matchbox cover

Real drawer stays inside cover

Real drawer removed

Dummy drawer shown empty

Pencil mark

① ②

Dummy concealed in cover

When you are ready to pick it up again, take it with your left hand at the sides, thumb to the right and fingers to the left. Put your left front finger at the left front corner so it slightly overlaps that edge. Bring your right hand behind the box and push in with that thumb to push the drawer out the front a little. Then with your left hand turn the box to the right until it is lengthwise. Now slowly pull the real drawer entirely out of the cover with your right hand. As you do that the first finger of your left hand, with its tip still over the edge at the corner, helps to keep the dummy drawer from sliding out. The dummy drawer remains hidden inside the cover.

With your left hand, put the lengthwise cover on the table and leave it there. The dummy drawer is well hidden within it because it is shorter than the cover. Whatever you secretly put into the box at the beginning is now in the full unfaked drawer that you hold in your right hand. You can just take it out to show it and toss the drawer aside on the table or you can hand the drawer to someone in the audience so he can remove what is in it.

The boxes of some brands of kitchen matches have tighter covers than others. If you find the double drawer doesn't slide easily enough through the cover you may want to trim a tiny edge off the top of both parts of the drawer, but that usually is not necessary.

Here are some tricks you can do with the box:

The Solitaire Addict

"My uncle was a great magician," you say as you pick up the matchbox. "We used to call him 'Uncle the Great.' Whenever he wasn't performing magic, he was always fooling around with a pack of cards."

You open the box, show it empty, close it and put it on

the table. "He was a solitaire addict. He used to sit and play solitaire by the hour—just to see how many trick moves he could make with the cards to beat himself at the game. But my aunt used to get burned up when he sat all night long playing solitaire."

You pick up the matchbox again. "One winter night she got so burned up that she built a fire in the fireplace and burned up his cards. Uncle the Great didn't say a word. He just took the box of matches from her, worked his magic—and produced another pack."

As you speak, you pull out what was the empty drawer, tip a pack of cards into your hand, spread them to show them to the audience, and then say, "And he sat right down again—and played a game of solitaire."

To set it up, all you need is a pack of cards hidden in the drawer of the box. In addition to being an amusing little trick in itself, this is an interesting way to lead into a routine of card tricks. After you produce the cards from the matchbox, shuffle them, and say, "I'd like to show you a few of the tricks my uncle taught me."

Safe Hiding Place

"Did you read about the magician whose apartment was burglarized?" you ask. "The thieves went through everything in the place—even the box of matches he had on his kitchen stove." You pick up the matchbox, dump out a few matches, and show that the box is otherwise empty. "But they didn't get away with much—and they were caught in a hurry when they tried to pawn a top hat they stole and a rabbit popped out of it."

You open the box again, put the cover on the table, and hold the drawer in your hand. "They didn't get his money because he remembered to make that invisible before he left the apartment that morning. The thieves had their hands right on it—but because it was invisible, they couldn't see it, of course." You turn over the drawer, dump a roll of dollar bills into your hand, toss the drawer aside on the table, and spread out the bills to show them. "As I said—he was a magician."

For this, you need half a dozen matches, several dollar bills or play money dollars, and a rubber band. Stack the bills together, fold them in half, put the rubber band around them to hold them flat, and hide them in the drawer of the matchbox. Pull out the dummy drawer a little and place the matches crosswise in the open end of it.

When you show the trick, pull open the dummy drawer, turn the whole box over to dump out the half-dozen matches, and show the drawer otherwise empty. Close the box, put it on your table, then pick it up again and remove the drawer and dump the roll of bills into your hand. Unsnap the rubber band, open out the fold, and fan the bills to display them.

THE TURN BOX

You show a box empty, inside and out and on all sides, and then magically produce half a dozen large handkerchiefs from it. The box itself is unfaked, but there is a hidden tube used with it, and the trick depends on the way the square-edged box and round tube are handled.

What you need:

An empty, standard-size facial tissue box, $4\frac{3}{4}''$ wide, $9\frac{3}{8}''$ long, and $2\frac{1}{2}''$ high.

The cardboard tube from the center of a roll of paper towels. This should be about $1\frac{1}{2}''$ in diameter.

Cloth adhesive tape, any color, 1½″ wide.

Self-adhesive decorative paper, preferably in a solid, bright-colored pattern.

A pencil, ruler, scissors, and a sharp knife or razor blade in a safety holder.

Six silk or compressible rayon handkerchiefs in various colors, each 18″ square.

How you make it:

Cut out and remove the entire top of the facial tissue box, the part with the oval opening. Cover all the inside and outside surfaces of the box with the self-adhesive decorative paper.

With the knife or razor blade in a holder, cut off a 5½″ section of the tube and discard the rest. Turn the small tube lengthwise and cut an opening in the center of one side of it, 1½″ long and 1″ across.

Cut off a 2″ piece of the cloth adhesive tape and turn it sticky side up. Take another piece of tape 3″ long and put that sticky side down on the first one, so the two pieces form a cross. Turn the attached pieces over with the non-sticky side of the smaller one upward. Press one end of the tube down upon it and bend the sticky part of the tape up to fasten it to the sides of the tube so as to seal off that end of the tube with a non-sticky surface at the inside. Take two more strips of tape and close off the opposite end of the tube the same way.

Cover the outside and both ends of the tube with pieces of the same self-adhesive decorative paper that was used to cover the box. Cut away the paper at the opening that was cut in the side of the tube and trim the edges around the opening.

The set-up:

Stuff one of the handkerchiefs into the tube until it is all inside except for one end. Twist that end several times around the end of a second handkerchief. Then push that into the tube, and so on, until all the handkerchiefs are inside. Turn the box mouth upward and drop the loaded tube into it so it lies lengthwise in the bottom. Have the box where you can carry it forward to your table to present the trick.

How you use it:

Carry the box forward and put it lengthwise at the center of your table, which should be cleared of other props. Stand behind and a little to the right of the table with your body turned slightly toward the left.

From now on the box is not lifted off the table until the end of the trick. One edge or one side of the box is always kept on the table as the box is turned backward or forward to show the audience various sides of it.

With your right hand at the right side of it, tilt the box over backward so what was the rear side is at the bottom and continue to tilt it toward you slightly until the rear edge is on the table. As you do that, bring your left hand behind the box, palm outward. Touch the tips of your left fingers to the table and your thumb to the top side of the box. The tube will roll out of the box toward you until it is stopped by rolling against your left fingers.

Close your left thumb on the box to hold it tipped back on its edge for a moment. Tap your right hand on the bottom of the box to indicate that it is solid. With your right hand, turn the box forward and over until it is upright on its bottom again and take both hands away. This has rolled the

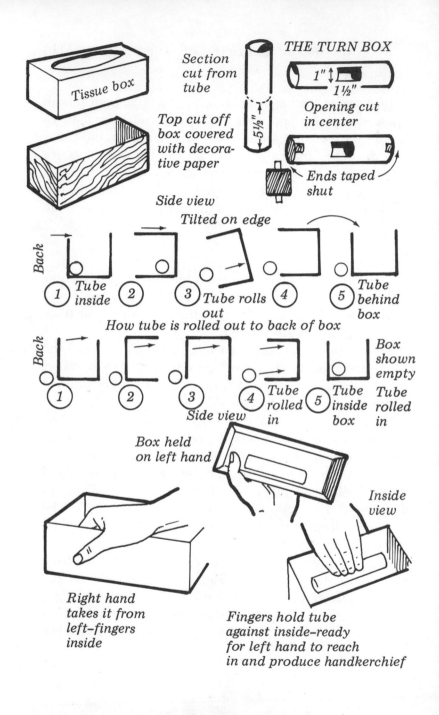

Tissue box

Section cut from tube

THE TURN BOX

1" 1½"

Top cut off box covered with decorative paper

Opening cut in center

Ends taped shut

Side view

Tilted on edge

Back

① *Tube inside* ② ③ *Tube rolls out* ④ ⑤ *Tube behind box*

How tube is rolled out to back of box

Back

① ② ③ ④ *Tube rolled in* ⑤ *Tube inside box* *Tube rolled in*

Box shown empty

Side view

Box held on left hand

Inside view

Right hand takes it from left–fingers inside

Fingers hold tube against inside–ready for left hand to reach in and produce handkerchief loaded tube out of the box so it now rests hidden behind it on the table.

With the box upright and the tube hidden in back of it, bring your left hand behind it, palm to the front and with the tips of those fingers touching the top of the table just back of the tube. Your thumb should rest lightly on the top rear edge of the box as if to steady it. That hand stays as it is during the rest of the turning of the box.

With your right hand turn the box forward to rest on the table so the audience can look inside it. Keep your left hand positioned as it was but bring that thumb down to hold the box. Tap the inside with your right hand to show the box empty. Then turn the box forward again with your right hand so the bottom is up. Close your left thumb down on the bottom and tap the front side with your right hand. Then turn it forward once more so the bottom is toward the audience and tap that with your right hand.

Your left thumb is on the top edge of the box and your fingers behind it. With a slight push of your fingers but without any movement of your left arm or of the box, just push the tube into the open side of the box.

As the tube rolls inside, immediately turn the box forward and upright with your right hand and for the first time lift the box up off the table. Bring the palm of your left hand up under the box so it rests on that hand. Hold it with your left hand under it, fingers to the front and thumb at the rear, and drop your right hand to your side.

The box rests upright on your left hand. Bring your right hand up to take the box so that your right fingers go down inside and press against the tube in the bottom and your thumb grips the box at the outside. Holding it that way, between your right thumb outside and fingers inside pressed to the tube, turn the box over from left to right until it is mouth down and shake it to show again that it is empty, and then turn it right to left so it is upright.

Show your left hand empty and reach inside the box as your right hand continues to hold it. With your left hand, pull the handkerchiefs out of the tube and the box one at a time and show them. Your right fingers are still inside the box to hold the tube steady in the bottom of it. When you have finished producing the handkerchiefs, your right hand puts the box aside.

Here's an example of the sort of a magical plot that can be built around the use of the box to make a more interesting trick of it than simply pulling out handkerchiefs:

A Crowd of Ghosts

For this you need two 18″ square white silk or rayon handkerchiefs and six white ones that are 12″ square. Tie the smaller ones together end to end in a chain and tuck those down into one side of the tube. Push one of the larger handkerchiefs into the other side of the tube except for its last end. Twist that several times around an end of the second large handkerchief and push that into the same side with the first one, leaving a small end sticking out. This is done so that after you pull out the first one the end of the second one will be drawn up and you won't mistake the string of small handkerchiefs for the larger ones.

Empty the right-hand pocket of your trousers and have the loaded tube lengthwise in the box.

"Ghosts can crowd themselves into the smallest spaces," you say as you bring forward the box and put it on your table. "They certainly beat humans when it comes to crowding into an elevator or into a bus." Tip the box backward to show the bottom and then upright with the tube hidden behind it. "Take this little box that I found in

an antique shop. The owner of the place said that it came
from a haunted house and that a ghost lived in the box."

Tip the box forward again and show the inside empty.
"How could a ghost ever get into a box this small? I didn't
believe it, of course." Tip it forward once more and tap the
side of it, and continue to turn it forward and over as you
speak, until the tube is loaded inside it. "But it made a good
story to tell my friends—only they didn't believe it either.
They said the owner of the antique shop really took
me—sold me an empty box."

Hold the box upright on your left hand. "But one night I
heard a skittering around in the box." Take it with your
right hand, shake it upside down, turn it upright and hold it.
"I didn't see anything at first. But when I looked again—
sure enough, there was a ghost."

Produce the first large white handkerchief and rest the
box on the table. "I caught it and put it into my pocket so I
could take it to show my friends." Roll up the handkerchief
and tuck it into the right-hand pocket of your trousers. As
your hand goes into the pocket, push the rolled handkerchief up into the top corner with your thumb so it stays
there and then take your hand out. "I don't know whether
the ghost didn't want to meet my friends or whether—being
a ghost—he just didn't want to be seen in public. Anyhow,
when I reached into my pocket to show them my ghost—he
was gone."

Reach into your pocket and grasp the bottom of the
lining. Pull it straight up, inside out, to show it to the audience. Your pocket will appear to be empty because the
rolled handkerchief will stay tucked out of sight in the top
corner of it. Push the pocket back in and remove your hand
and show it empty.

"My friends decided that I never did have a ghost in my
pocket," you say. "They're skeptical, I'm afraid. Some

people don't believe in ghosts. What happened, of course, is that he just went back home—into his box."

Pick up the box with your right fingers inside to hold the tube, and with your left hand produce the duplicate large handkerchief from it. "He still lives there. I've gotten to know him pretty well. Ghosts are nice pets to have—you never have to feed them. Not only can one ghost crowd into a space as small as this . . . I've discovered that he has his whole family living there with him!"

As you speak, pull out the string of small white handkerchiefs and hold them spread between your hands to show the ghost's "whole family."

MAKE MINE ORANGE JUICE

There is a carton of orange juice and an empty glass on a tray on your table. You cover them for a moment and the juice carton changes into a milk carton. Then it changes back again. Meanwhile, the glass, which repeatedly has been shown empty, suddenly becomes filled with orange juice.

What you need:

An empty one-quart waxed pasteboard orange juice carton and an empty one-quart milk carton.

Two identical heavy-bottomed drinking glasses, each about 2½" in diameter and 5½" tall.

Enough orange drink or orange-colored water to fill one of the glasses. (Water can be colored orange with kitchen food coloring.)

A large brown paper bag, about 12" by 17", the kind used to package groceries at supermarket checkout counters.

A tray on which to stand the carton and glasses.

Strong adhesive or glue, such as one of the white "craft" glues (not paper paste or rubber cement).

A sharp pointed knife and a pair of scissors.

How you make it:

The bottom must be cleanly cut from the orange juice carton. Start by making a hole in the center of the bottom with the knife and enlarge the hole until you can get the scissors into it. Then cut away small pieces, working out toward the edges, but be careful not to cut into the sides of the carton. Cut out the entire bottom and trim off the edges evenly so the carton will stand upright.

The next step is to cut two attached sides from the milk carton so that you have what amounts to a diagonal half of the carton without a bottom. You want two full adjoining panels, including the flap parts that fold in at the top. Choose two with the word "milk" printed on them in large letters, not the sides with mostly small print.

That two-paneled piece of the milk carton has to be glued over two adjoining sides of the orange juice carton. It should cover the two sides that have small print on them, not the sides with the main labels. Coat the inside of the piece from the milk carton and both outside surfaces of the juice carton liberally with glue, especially along all edges and at the top and bottom. Glue the two parts firmly together, wipe off the excess glue, and allow the finished carton to dry thoroughly before using it.

If you stand it upright on a table so the diagonal corner is directly toward the front, you should have what looks like a milk carton. Turned completely around so the other diagonal corner faces front, it looks like a carton of orange juice. When it is placed in either position, the angles of visibility are very deceptive. Anyone seated in front, or even fairly close at either side, should not be able to see the rear of the carton.

Cut the large paper bag across from side to side to remove the bottom part of it so that what you have left is a bottomless bag about 12" wide and 13" high. Trim the bottom edges squarely so it will stand upright by itself when it is opened out. When you are performing the trick this is put over the carton and glass as a screen. It is bottomless so that you can simply lift it off, which would not be possible if you used a bag with a bottom in it.

The set-up:

Fill one of the glasses with orange liquid and put it on the tray toward the left-hand side as you stand behind the table. Cover that glass with the bottomless carton, turned so its orange juice sides diagonally face the audience. Put the empty glass to the right of it. Open out the bottomless bag and put it over both the glass and the carton.

How you use it:

This should be performed slowly. First you say a few words, then handle the things as explained, then speak the next line and remain silent while you perform the next action, and so on, allowing time so the audience becomes aware of each of the magical changes.

Stand to the right of your table. With your left hand, lift the bag straight up and off the glass and carton and keep it in that hand. Say, "Some people like orange juice for breakfast."

With your right hand, point to the carton of orange juice. Then pick up the glass, turn it upside down to show it empty and replace it where it was, but don't say anything about the glass. Hold the paper bag open between both hands and put it back over the carton and glass.

MAKE MINE ORANGE JUICE

Bottom cut out of juice carton

Two side panels with top flaps cut from milk carton

Piece from milk carton glued to sides of juice carton

Audience view

Turned diagonally this way looks like milk

Turned around diagonally looks like orange juice

Bottomless bag serves as a covering screen

Bottom cut off large paper bag

(1) Full glass hidden inside carton empty glass beside it

(2) Inside bag carton lifted off one glass put down over other

(3) Empty glass now hidden inside carton full glass beside it

Put your right hand inside as if to straighten the paper. With your fingers inside, tap the right side of the paper. Then bring that hand over toward the left. Take the top of the carton and give it a complete turn so the milk sides of the carton are now diagonally toward the audience. There is no need to hurry the hidden turning of the carton. Look down inside and make sure it is positioned properly. Straighten the left side of the bag a little and remove your hand.

"Of course, there are other people who prefer milk," you say. Lift off the paper bag and show that the orange juice carton has changed to a milk carton. Again without saying anything about the glass, pick it up, turn it upside down, right it and replace it on the tray, *a little toward the rear* but where it will still be in view of the audience. Cover the things with the paper bag again.

Reach down inside with your left hand as you say, "Milk?" With that hand inside, turn the carton so the orange juice sides are toward the front. When it is turned, lift the carton straight up into view, almost but not completely out of the top of the bag. Show that it has become a juice carton again and say, "Or orange juice?"

You have lifted the carton off the full glass that was hidden inside it. Now as you put the carton back down inside the paper bag, put it over the empty glass so that one will be hidden within it. As far as the audience knows, there is only one glass, but the filled one is now ready to be revealed.

"Personally I always like to start the day with orange juice," you say as you lift the paper bag and "discover" the glass full of juice beside the carton. "Oh, how nice—somebody has just poured me a big glassful."

Lift the glass, shake it a little so the liquid moves around in it, display it to the audience, and then put it back on the tray. Cover everything with the paper bag.

(Remember when you lift away your tray to clear the table that there are two glasses on it and one is filled with liquid. Carry it carefully to avoid a spill.)

THE PORTABLE WELL

To a magician a "well" is an opening in the top of a table with a bag under it, used to secretly drop things into it so they will fall out of sight. This one requires no special table. It can be put to use anywhere.

As the audience sees it, you put a decorated box on the table and take from the box various things you are using to perform some particular trick. Apparently to give the audience a better view, you turn the box over and stand those things on the bottom of it. Right in back of whatever you put on display, there is a concealed hole in the bottom of the box that serves as a well.

What you need:
A cardboard gift box about 5¼" square.
A piece of cloth about 6½" square. This can be cut from an old pocket handkerchief or any scrap material. Color doesn't matter since it won't be seen.
Adhesive package sealing tape, 1½" wide.
Black cloth adhesive tape, 1½" wide.
Yellow cloth adhesive tape, ¾" wide.
A pencil, ruler, and pair of scissors.

How you make it:
Turn the box bottom up on a table. Measure in ¼" from the edge nearest you and ½" in from each of the other three

THE PORTABLE WELL 1

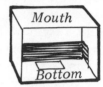

½"   ½"

¼"   ¼"

(1) *Marking off bottom*

(2) *Cut out*

(3) *Black tape along this edge and under box to inside*

MEASURING AND CUTTING

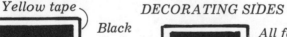

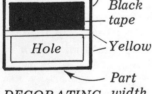

Mouth

Mouth

Bottom — Mouth

Mouth — Bottom

One edge of cloth fastened to one side—inside center

Cloth fastened across inside center

Box turned bottom up anything dropped through hole lands on cloth

Inside box

Box mouth up—black tape at back and sides above hole in bottom

FASTENING CLOTH INSIDE

DECORATING SIDES

Yellow tape

Black tape

Yellow

Hole

Part width of tape bent over outside to side of box

DECORATING BOTTOM OF BOX

All four sides decorated same as bottom—two black panels—yellow around and across center

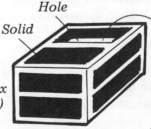

Hole

Solid

Strips of tape inside make hole look like black panel

Finished box (bottom up)

Audience view

edges and draw pencil lines to mark off those margins around the bottom of the box. Next measure from the edge nearest you to the exact center of the bottom. Draw a horizontal pencil line straight across the center from side to side.

With the scissors, cut through the bottom of the box horizontally along that center line until you come to the ½" margin marked at the right. Cut vertically down along the pencil line at that side to the margin that is marked at the edge nearest you. Then cut to the left horizontally until you reach the margin marked at the left edge of the box. Cut vertically up along the left margin to the center and remove the cut-out piece.

You should have an oblong opening in the bottom of the box, from its center to within ½" of both sides and ¼" of the nearest edge. Cut off a 4¼" length of black cloth tape. Fasten it lengthwise along the cut edge of the opening nearest to you and bend the remainder of its width down inside the hole to fasten it underneath at the inside of the box.

Turn the box mouth upward. Cut off a 5¼" length of black cloth tape and fasten its edge right over the edge of the piece you previously attached so that the new piece runs across lengthwise inside the box from one side to the other. Fasten a second piece of tape the same length just above the first one, so it overlaps it slightly, then a third piece above those. Where those strips end, at *each* side of the inside of the box, attach three slightly overlapping lengthwise strips each 3" long.

The piece of cloth acts as a "net" inside the box to catch anything dropped into the opening in the bottom so it won't fall all the way through and thump on the table. It has to be attached to all four sides of the box so it hangs across the middle to divide the inside of the box into upper and lower sections. That is done by fastening the cloth to the sides with package sealing tape.

With the box still mouth up, slide the ruler inside it against the side that is away from you. Measure down about 2″ from the top and make a pencil mark. Hold one edge of the piece of cloth on a line with the mark and fasten that edge to that side with a horizontal strip of the package tape. Bring the opposite edge of the cloth over to the side nearest you, fasten that, and then fasten the other edges of cloth to the remaining sides of the box. Reinforce all the strips with additional tape, gathering a little of the material under them as you seal them so the cloth is firmly held. When the box is turned bottom up, the center of the cloth should hang rather loosely inside but should be well above the table.

That completes the actual construction of the box, but it must be decorated with strips of tape that will cover all its surfaces in a particular way to help conceal the opening. The illusion is partly visual, based on what magicians call the "black art" principle, but the repeated design also has a psychological effect. Looking at the repeated pattern on the sides, viewers will assume the bottom must be the same.

Turn the box bottom up with the hole at the side toward you. Fasten a strip of the yellow ¾″ tape lengthwise along the outer margin marked at that edge, but don't bend any of it over inside the hole. Since the margin is ¼″ wide, part of the width of the tape will extend out over the outer edge of the box. Bend that part down to fasten it to the side. At the center of the box, just beyond the hole, fasten another lengthwise strip of yellow tape across from side to side.

Now take the 1½″ black tape. Fasten a strip of that across lengthwise from side to side directly beyond the strip of yellow so the edge of the black touches the edge of the yellow. Then attach another yellow strip lengthwise along the margin of the box at the far edge, touching along the black strip at the other side of it. Cover the margin at the left side edge of the box with a vertical strip of yellow tape, all the way down that edge from the far side of the box to the side nearest you, and cover the margin along the right side edge the same way.

The result should be that the entire bottom of the box is decorated with tape so that none of the original bottom of the box itself shows through. There is a border of yellow around the margins at all four sides, a panel of black, a yellow strip across the center, and then the hole in the box instead of a matching panel of black. If there are any places that the edges of the tapes do not cover, overlap them with additional strips of tape the same color.

The four sides of the box each should be decorated in a similar way, each with two panels of black surrounded by yellow side borders, and with a yellow strip across the center. Overlap the tapes at the corners and edges.

Turn the box bottom up with the hole side away from you. Sit in a chair about eight feet back from the table, which probably is closer than any member of your audience would be. The hole in the bottom of the box appears to be one of the black panels of decoration. What you really see is the black tape that is fastened to the back of the inside of the box just beneath the hole. The fact that you stand things on the bottom of the box in front of the hole to display them adds to the deception and the box is handled so that the audience should have no reason to suspect that there is a hole in the bottom.

The set-up:

There are many ways to use a well in a table, and most of them can be adapted to the use of this portable well in a box, within the size limits of whatever will fit inside it. To understand the basic handling, first turn the box bottom up with its opening toward you, then turn it over from left to right so it is mouth up.

Push down the cloth that is across the center inside the box and rest some small object such as a ping-pong ball on it. Have the box on a chair or someplace else near your table.

How you use it:

Pick up the box with your right hand at the top rear edge. Keep that hand there to hold it and bring your left hand under the box so the bottom rests on the palm of that hand, which covers the hole. Carry the box to the table and put it down.

Reach into the box, remove the ball, and place it at the front of the table. Turn the box over on the table from left to right so it is bottom up. Pick up the ball, display it, and rest it on the solid part of the bottom in front of the hole. You apparently put it there so the audience has a better view of it.

Stand a little to the right of the table. Bring your right hand, with the back of it toward the audience, down in front of the ball as if to cup your hand around it and pick it up. The little finger of your cupped hand should touch against the box.

Move your hand back, shielding the ball from view as it falls into the well. Close your fingers as if they held the ball, hold your hand high, and walk forward a few steps away from the table. Rub your fingers together and then slowly open them and show that the ball has vanished.

With a Handkerchief

Put a folded pocket handkerchief inside the box with the ball. Carry the box to the table as before. Take out the ball

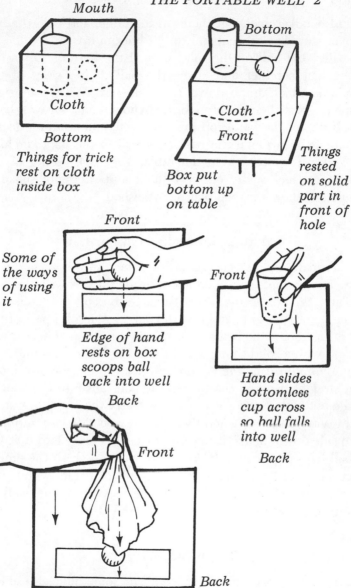

Mouth

Cloth

Bottom

Things for trick rest on cloth inside box

Bottom

Cloth

Front

Box put bottom up on table

Things rested on solid part in front of hole

Some of the ways of using it

Front

Edge of hand rests on box scoops ball back into well

Back

Front

Hand slides bottomless cup across so ball falls into well

Back

Back

Front

Ball falls into well from handkerchief

Back

and handkerchief, put them on the table, and turn the box over from left to right to bring it bottom up.

Rest the ball on the solid part of the bottom. Open out the handkerchief and cover the ball so the sides of the handkerchief drape down over the box. With your right hand, grasp the ball through the handkerchief. Draw it back a little, let the ball drop into the well, and continue to lift your hand up as if the ball were still in the handkerchief. Walk a few steps from the table. Take one corner of the handkerchief with your left hand and suddenly shake it open to show that the ball has vanished.

With a Bottomless Cup or Bag

Prepare a paper cup by cutting the entire bottom out of it. Turn it on its side and have it inside the box with the ball. Carry the box to the table. Remove the cup and ball, turn the box bottom up, and rest the cup on the solid part of the bottom. Show the ball and drop it into the cup, where it will land with a solid thump because of the box that is under it.

Without lifting the bottom of the cup from the box, move it straight back off the box so the ball falls into the well as the bottomless cup passes over it. Carry the cup a few steps away from the table and then turn it over sidewise until it is upside down. Shake it to show that it is empty and that the ball has disappeared. If you wish, you can crush the empty cup in your hands and toss it to the floor behind you.

A bottomless paper bag can be used with the well to vanish a variety of small objects in the same way.

The Rip-apart Tube

For this novel vanish of a ball or something else about that size, you will need a sheet of typing paper or an 8″ by

11″ piece of newspaper. Roll it into a tube with a diameter large enough to take the ball or whatever you want to vanish and fasten the outside of the tube together with a strip of transparent tape near the top end and another near the bottom.

With the scissors, cut an opening slightly larger than the diameter of the ball at the center of one side of the tube. Be careful not to cut through the front of the tube. Stand the paper tube inside the box, with the hole in the tube toward the back, and have the ball in the box with it. Have the box on your table at the start.

Pick up the tube with your left hand so your palm comes against the hole and covers it. Hold it vertically, with the ends top and bottom. With your right hand, remove the ball, put it on the table, and turn the box over sidewise to bring it bottom up.

Turn your left hand around, still covering the hole in the tube with your palm, as you show all sides of the tube to the audience, then turn the back of it toward the rear. Take the top end of the upright tube with your right hand and bring your left hand, palm upward, under the bottom end. Close your left fingers up around the bottom end to hold the tube.

Pick up the ball with your right hand, display it, and drop it into the top of the tube. Place the palm of your right hand over the top end. Holding the tube between your two hands, bring it down to rest it lengthwise on the bottom of the box right across the well. As you pretend to adjust the tube so it will not roll off the box, give it a half turn and tilt it slightly so the ball falls down into the well. Leave the tube lying there for a moment.

Then take it up as before, with the palms of your two hands against the ends of it, keeping the hole in the tube to the rear. Step forward and suddenly crush the tube flat between your hands. Quickly rip the paper several times, toss the pieces into the air, and show your hands empty.

Here's another unusual trick that makes use of the portable well:

Big Bargain Offer

"Time for a commercial," you say as you carry the box to your table. "For all the women in the audience who like to sew their own clothes, I have a special sensational bargain offer—more than one hundred and fifty yards of the finest cotton material, guaranteed in perfect condition, for just one dollar. Can you believe it? One hundred and fifty yards of best quality cotton for just one buck." You turn to one of the women spectators. "If you heard an offer like that, would you go for it? . . . Well, here's exactly what you'd get . . ."

From the box, you remove a large spool of thread. "That's right—one hundred and fifty yards of cotton . . . one spool of thread." You turn the box bottom up and stand the spool on it. "I'll bet if somebody tricked you that way, you'd demand your money back, wouldn't you?" You pick up the spool of thread and hold it in your closed hand. "So would I—only quicker. I'd just take the spool . . . and change it into a dollar bill." As you speak, you open your hand. The spool has vanished and in its place you have a dollar bill.

You need a large spool of bright-colored thread for this and a dollar bill or a play-money dollar. The bill must be rolled up very tightly. Put it on a table, fold over one tiny edge, press it down with both thumbs, and continue to roll and flatten the bill at each turn. Push the rolled bill into the center hole of the spool as far as it will go without coming out the other side. Bend down the part of the bill that still sticks out of the spool and flatten that with your thumb against the top of the spool. Put the spool in the box so the top of it where the bill sticks out is toward the right and have the box on your table.

Tell about the "special offer." Reach into the box with your left hand. Grip the spool between your thumb and first finger so your thumb comes over the bent part of the bill and holds it flat against the top of the spool to hide it. Hold up the spool to display it and let it be seen that there is nothing else in your hand. With your right hand, turn the box over sidewise and bottom up.

Turn the back of your left hand toward the audience. With that thumb, press the end of the bill against the inside of your fingers. Take the spool with your right hand by drawing it out of your left hand, which holds back the bill so it pulls out of the spool and remains hidden in that hand. Drop your left hand to your side, with your fingers loosely curled around the hidden bill. With your right hand, stand the spool on the bottom of the box in front of the well.

Go on talking about it for a moment. Then bring your cupped left hand, which still hides the bill, in front of the spool. Pretend to close your hand around the spool as you move it back and let it drop into the well. Hold your hand high, move away from the table, and bring your right hand to your left. Take one edge of the bill and draw it out of your left hand so it unrolls and is fully opened. Show the bill and show that your hands are otherwise empty and the spool has vanished.

RING A ROD

A finger ring is borrowed from someone in the audience and dropped into an envelope which is sealed and stood in full view on the table. You show a small cardboard tube and wooden rod. The rod is pushed through the tube and the ends of the rod are rested on the bottoms of two upturned tumblers so the tube hangs suspended between them.

You tear the envelope into pieces and scatter the scraps from your hand so they flutter down over the tube. The ring has vanished. Then you tap the tube to one side of the rod. The missing ring suddenly appears hanging on the rod between the two tumblers.

What you need:

A wooden dowel stick, 14″ long and ⅜″ in diameter.

The cardboard tube from the center of a roll of bathroom tissue. This should be 4″ long and ½″ in diameter. You want one that is plain cardboard with no advertising printed on it.

Two flat-bottomed plastic tumblers.

A small piece of poster board or other cardboard, about 3″ square.

White cloth adhesive tape, ¾″ wide.

A package of manila coin envelopes, 2½″ by 4¼″, the kind with a flap that opens at one end. One of these envelopes will be used each time you perform the trick.

A pencil, scissors, and a ruler.

A small curtain ring or finger ring, about ¾″ in diameter, to use for practice.

How you make it:

Put the small piece of cardboard on a table. Stand the tube upright on the center of it. Draw a circle on the cardboard around the bottom end of the tube and put the tube aside. Cut out the circle *inside* the pencil line and then trim the edge of it slightly all the way around so that you have a cardboard disc just a little smaller than the circumference of the tube. The disc should be small enough so that it can be pushed flat inside the tube without bending.

Measure in ½" from one side of the disc and draw a pencil line between that point and the edge. Measure up ½" from that and draw a parallel line out to the edge. Draw a vertical line to connect the two at their inner ends. Cut out the cardboard between the lines so there is an opening ½" wide and ½" deep at one side of the disc.

The disc has to be fastened flatly across the inside of the tube at its center. Take a 2" length of the cloth adhesive tape and fasten one end of that to the disc just beyond the inner edge of the opening that was cut in the side of it. Loosely roll the other end of that tape upon itself so it is clear of the edge. Take another piece of tape 3" long, place that across the disc so the center of it is fastened to it, and roll both its ends loosely in upon themselves. Hold the disc in your hand, turn it over, and apply two strips of tape in the same way to the reverse side, rolling the ends of the tapes upon themselves so the edges of the disc are clear.

To position the disc inside the center of the tube, take the tube in your left hand and push the first two fingers of that hand up inside the tube to the middle. With your right hand, push the disc down inside from the top until its bottom rests flat on the tips of those two fingers. Work your right first finger down inside the top of the tube and open out the rolled ends of tape so as to fasten them firmly to the inside of the tube. Then turn the tube over so the other end is up and work your finger inside to fasten those ends of tape.

You should now have a tube with a flat disc fastened across the center. If you drop a finger ring into the top of the tube, it won't fall on through and out the bottom because the opening cut in the disc is too small for the ring to pass through. But you can easily push the wooden dowel rod through because its diameter is smaller than the opening in the center disc.

Prepare one of the envelopes by trimming a tiny edge off its bottom end, cutting straight across it with the scissors. That leaves it bottomless so that a ring dropped into the top will fall right through the envelope into your hand unless the bottom end is held pinched together.

Hold the bottomless envelope upright with its flap end at the top. Squeeze its sides together to flatten it in that direction. Slightly crease the envelope down the center and then open it out again to its original shape. The creasing helps to puff it out a little so it won't look flat when there is supposed to be a ring inside it.

The set-up:

Push the rod through the tube so the tube is at the center of it and put them lengthwise on your performing table. Place the envelope, back upward and with its flap closed and the flap end toward the audience, on the table in front of the tube and rod. Stack the two plastic tumblers together and stand them bottoms up at the rear of the table to the right. Put the ring you are using for practice on the seat of a chair so you can pretend a member of the audience is sitting there. (If you wish, all the props can be on a small tray so you can carry them together to and from the table.)

How you use it:

Stand behind the table. Pick up the plastic tumblers, show them and stand them bottoms up, one at each side of the table and about a foot apart. Pick up the rod with your right hand at the right end of it. Hold it lengthwise and twirl the tube around on it. Then tilt it down to the left and bring up your left hand to take the tube as it slides off the rod.

Hold the tube upright with your hand about six inches above the top of the table. With your right hand, push the bottom end of the rod down into the tube until it is past the

RING A ROD

³/₈" Diameter rod

Opening cut in disc — ½"

Strips of tape fastened to both faces — ← 2" → 3"

Ends of tape rolled in to clear edges

Disc fastened across inside center of tube

Passes through opening

Tube hangs suspended between tumblers

Bottom edge trimmed off envelope

Left hand takes it— ring drops from envelope into hand

Left hand takes tube from rod

Right hand holds envelope with bottom pinched shut

Left hand drops to side hiding ring in fingers

Bottom of tube goes over hidden ring

Tube hangs at right end of rod— sharply tapped to left

Ring appears on rod

opening in the disc and then let the rod drop until its end strikes the table, but not so it falls all the way out of the tube.

Turn the rod lengthwise with the tube on it. Take one end in each hand and tilt the rod up and down a few times so the tube slides back and forth and then tilt it to bring the tube about to the center. Rest the two ends of the rod on the bottoms of the tumblers so the tube hangs suspended between them.

Ask to borrow a ring from someone in the audience and have the person hold it up for everyone to see. Pick up the envelope, casually show both sides, and then hold it upright by pinching the bottom end of it between your right thumb and first finger. Close your other fingers out of the way so the audience has a clear view of the envelope. The back of it should be toward you.

Keep it held that way with your right hand as you go to the person who offered the ring. With your left hand, open the flap, squeeze the sides to open the envelope wide, and ask the person to drop the ring into it. Drop your left hand to your side, hold the envelope high with your right hand, and return to your table with it. (For practice, pick up the ring from the chair with your left hand and drop it into the envelope, held as explained.)

You are still holding the envelope gripped at the bottom edge between your right thumb and first finger, with the back of it toward you and the flap open at the top. Bring your left hand over to take it, with the back of that hand toward the audience. Grip it at the bottom so your left thumb is at the rear across the bottom edge, pressing that edge against the first two fingers of your left hand. Cup the other fingers of that hand loosely beneath it. Lift the envelope to your mouth, lick the flap, and lower your hand again.

Bring your right hand to the top of the envelope to press the flap shut and seal it. As you do that, release the pressure of your left thumb so the ring secretly falls out the bottom of the envelope into your slightly cupped left hand. Lift the envelope away with your right hand and drop your left hand to your side with your fingers loosely curled to keep the ring hidden in that hand.

Pay no attention to that hand. Look at the sealed envelope your right hand is holding. With your right hand, rest the envelope against the tumbler at the right side of the table and leave it there in full view. Then pick up the rod with that hand and lift it and the tube from the tumblers.

Tilt the lengthwise rod up a little and spin the tube around on it. Tilt it down to the left and bring your left hand up from your side to take the tube as it slides off the rod. The tube goes into your left hand so the bottom end of it comes right over the ring that is hidden in your fingers.

Tap the side of the tube with the rod that is in your right hand and at the same time turn your left hand over so the ring secretly slides down into the tube until it is stopped by the disc at the center. The tapping covers any slight sound the ring may make falling into the tube.

Now you seem to repeat what you did at the start of the trick to "prove" that the tube is empty. With your left hand, hold the tube upright about six inches above the top of the table. Glance down into it to see where the opening is in the disc and tilt the tube a little to that side so the ring slides over the opening. With your right hand, push the vertical rod down inside the tube so it goes through the ring and the opening. Release the top end of the rod so it falls through and the bottom end strikes the table, but not so the rod falls all the way out of the tube.

Turn the rod with the tube on it to the right so they are lengthwise. Rest the two ends of the rod on the bottoms of the tumblers so the tube hangs suspended between them.

Hold your left hand over the left end of the rod to steady it. With your right hand, slowly slide the tube along the length of the rod, all the way to the right until it is next to the tumbler at that side. As you slide the tube, the disc inside automatically pulls the ring along with it toward that end, keeping it hidden inside the tube and giving the audience a clear view of the empty length of the rod. Leave the tube there, suspended on the rod near its right end.

Pick up the empty envelope that supposedly contains the ring. Tear it in half, in half again, and once more. Hold the scraps in your right hand about a foot above the rod and tube and drop them from your hand so they flutter down. Show both hands empty. The ring has vanished.

Place your left hand over the bottom of the tumbler at that side to hold the end of the rod steady. Tap the right bottom edge of the tube sharply with the first finger of your right hand so the tube slides across the rod to the left, revealing the ring that now hangs in view on the rod.

Take the extreme right end of the rod between your right first finger and thumb. Lift the rod, hold it lengthwise, and with your left hand remove the tube from the rod and place it upright on the table. Take the extreme left end of the rod between your left first finger and thumb. Tilt the rod up and down so the ring slides back and forth on it. Holding the rod that way, go to the person in the audience and return the borrowed ring.

5

❦

GADGETS
AND GIMMICKS

THUMB SLING COIN

With the help of this gimmick you can catch coins from the
air or perform various close-up coin tricks that appear to be
clever sleight of hand. It is a coin with a ring of clear plastic
attached to the back so that the tip of your thumb fits into
it. The plastic ring is "custom made" to fit the size of your
own thumb and the device can be put together in a few
seconds, using a real half-dollar or any coin that size.

What you need:

A clear self-adhesive plastic sheet, about 4″ by 6″.
Sometimes called "plastic sandwich" sheets, these are made
for protecting cards, clippings, and photos and are available
at most photo supply counters.

A half-dollar or coin of that size.

A pencil, scissors, and a ruler.

How you make it:

Turn the plastic sheet face down, narrow ends top and
bottom. Measure down about ½″ from the top edge and

142   BILL SEVERN'S MAGIC WORKSHOP

draw a horizontal pencil line across the sheet's protective backing. Cut off that ½″ strip and put aside the rest of the sheet.

Lay the coin on the table. Peel the backing from the self-adhesive plastic strip. Put the strip, sticky side down, horizontally across the center of the coin, so that an equal length of plastic extends beyond each side of the coin.

Place the tip of your right thumb on the center of the coin. Bend the left end of the strip over your thumb. Then bend the right end of the strip over upon that to fasten the two together so that the tip of your thumb fits inside rather snugly. The rear edge of the plastic ring should come just about to the rear of your thumbnail.

Press down with your thumb on the part that is fastened to the coin. Then slide your thumb out and press down hard with your first finger to cement the ring tightly to the coin.

Because of the adhesive used on these plastic sheets, the little thumb sling should remain quite firmly fixed to the coin for a considerable time even with a lot of handling. But it is wise to test it each time before using it. If the plastic strip has worked loose, it is easy enough to replace it with a new one.

Unlike a band of transparent tape, which incidentally will *not* work well for this, the plastic holds its shape. You can easily slide your thumb in and out of the sling without fumbling and it always exactly fits your own thumb.

The set-up:

Depending on how you intend to use it, you can have the sling coin lying behind something on your table where you can slide your thumb into it in picking up the other object, or you can have it in the right-hand pocket of your jacket or trousers where you can get it on your thumb as you take it from your pocket as you would any other coin.

THUMB SLING COIN 1

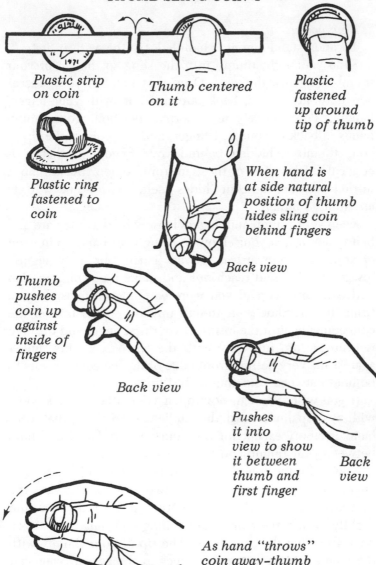

Plastic strip
on coin

Thumb centered
on it

Plastic
fastened
up around
tip of thumb

Plastic ring
fastened to
coin

When hand is
at side natural
position of thumb
hides sling coin
behind fingers

Back view

Thumb
pushes
coin up
against
inside of
fingers

Back view

Pushes
it into
view to show
it between
thumb and
first finger

Back
view

As hand "throws"
coin away–thumb
slides it down be-
hind fingers again

Back view

How you use it:

To understand how it is handled, try this with it first:

Slide your right thumb into the sling so the tip of your thumb is against the coin. Drop that hand to your side as you naturally would, back outward and with your fingers hanging down loosely in a normal position. Your thumb hangs in back of your first finger, and the coin at the tip of your thumb is hidden behind your fingers so that it is concealed from view of those in front. When your thumb is in that position, the coin "hides itself," with no need to do anything to hide it.

Keep your thumb and fingers loosely held as they are and bend your arm at your elbow to bring your hand up in front of you, back outward as it was. Turn your body slightly toward the left and reach out and make a catching motion with your fingers as if you were catching an invisible coin from the air. Slide your thumb upward so the face of the coin comes against the inside of your first finger and the coin is brought into full view with the tip of your first finger against the very bottom front edge of it. The coin appears to be held between your thumb and finger.

If you wish, you can now open your other fingers wide, with your palm toward the audience, to show that your hand is empty except for the coin you produced and hold between your thumb and finger.

Now, with the coin still in view between your thumb and finger, turn your hand as before, with its back toward the audience. Make a throwing motion toward the left and slightly toward the rear, straightening your fingers as if you were throwing the coin away. The tip of your thumb, with the coin attached, naturally comes to the rear of your first and second fingers, so that it is again hidden from view.

Drop your hand to your side with your thumb and fingers hanging down normally as at the start.

You have caught a coin from the air and made it disappear. Reach down behind your right knee, slide the coin to the tip of your fingers, and bring it out to show it again. Bring your hand up in front of you, display the coin, and "throw it away" once more. Reach up to the lobe of your right ear, tug it between your thumb and finger, and slide the coin into view as you seem to pluck it from your ear.

Hold your hand in front of you with the coin in view between your thumb and finger. Bring your left hand over and take the very top edge of the coin between your left first finger and thumb. Pull the coin straight up so the sling slides off your right thumb, and drop your right hand to your side. Show the coin for a moment with your left hand and then put it away in your left-hand pocket.

A Close-up Routine with the Sling Coin

Have the coin in a right-hand pocket so you can get your thumb into the sling in taking it out. Remove the coin from your pocket and display it between your thumb and first finger. Hold your left hand palm upward in front of you.

With your right hand, touch the bottom edge of the coin to the center of your left palm as if you were putting the coin into your left hand. Close up your left fingers, and as you do, draw your thumb and the attached coin up behind your right fingers. Take your right hand away and drop it to your side. Hold your closed left hand as though it still contained the coin. After a moment, slowly open your fingers and show that it has vanished.

Bring your right hand, back outward, up to the bottom

edge of the right-hand lapel of your jacket so your thumb slides up under the lapel and your fingers are over the outside of it. Continue to slide your hand upward a few inches. Press the tip of your right first finger against the outside of the lapel so it is directly over the tip of your thumb, which is hiding the coin beneath the lapel.

Open out your other fingers so it can be seen that there is nothing in your hand as your lapel is gripped between your first finger on top and your thumb underneath. Pull your thumb and first finger straight out to the right, away from your lapel, and the coin will suddenly appear between them.

Show the coin and bend down to bring it against the front of your left leg just above your knee. Hold it there between your first finger and thumb so the face of the coin is outward. With your left hand, gather a little of the material of your trousers and fold that over the coin. As the cloth covers it, draw the coin behind your fingers with your right thumb. Take that hand away and let it hang naturally at your side. Your left first finger holds the cloth folded against your leg as if the coin were still inside the fold. Lift your left finger, the cloth unfolds, and the coin has vanished again.

Lift your left foot, reach down to the heel of it with your right hand, and thumb the coin into view between your finger and thumb as if you were pulling it from the heel of your shoe. Show the coin, secretly slide your thumb back out of the sling, and drop the coin into your cupped left hand. With that hand, put it away in your pocket.

Rising Coin Through Envelope

You drop a coin into an envelope. The coin rises up through it, slowly seeming to penetrate it, until it finally balances itself on the envelope's very top edge.

For this, in addition to the sling coin, you will need an ordinary envelope, personal-letter size, not the long kind used for business letters. Have the empty envelope in one of the inside pockets of your jacket and the sling coin in a right-hand pocket.

Take out the envelope, casually show both sides, and turn it lengthwise with the flap side toward those who are watching. Open the envelope and hold the flap at the top between your left thumb and first finger so the envelope hangs down from its flap.

Reach into your pocket with your right hand, slide your thumb into the sling, and bring out the coin to show it between your thumb and first finger. Put that hand down into the envelope as if to leave the coin there, but inside the envelope slide the coin up behind your fingers. Immediately take your hand out with the coin hidden on your thumb. Grasp the right-hand side edge of the envelope between that thumb at the back and your fingers in front.

Hold the envelope that way with your right hand and close down the flap with your left hand. Keep your right hand as it is, and with your left hand turn the top edge of the envelope down to the left. That pivots it between your right finger and thumb so the right-side edge of the envelope is brought to the top. Drop your left hand to your side.

You are now holding the envelope, with its narrow end at the top, between your right fingers in front and thumb in the rear. The face of the hidden coin is against the rear of the envelope. Behind the envelope, slide your thumb and the coin as far to the left as you can. Then very slowly slide your thumb upward, gradually pushing the coin into view, until its bottom edge rises to rest on the very top edge of the envelope.

It should appear to those watching as if the coin somehow

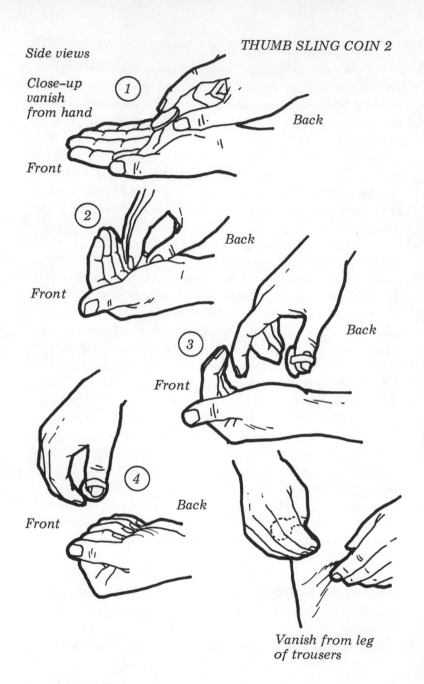

Side views

Close-up vanish from hand

THUMB SLING COIN 2

① Back

Front

② Back

Front

③ Back

Front

④ Back

Front

Vanish from leg of trousers

rose up inside the envelope, penetrated it, and continued to rise up through the top until it came to balance itself on the edge. Hold it that way for a moment. Then bring your left hand over in front of the coin to take it. As your left hand covers it to take the coin between its first finger and thumb, slide your right thumb free of the sling and down behind the envelope. Show the coin with your left hand and put it away in your pocket. Let the envelope fall from your right hand and flutter down empty to the floor.

Six Halves and a Dollar

You catch a half-dollar from the air with your right hand, take it with your left hand, and put it away in your pocket. You produce four more half-dollars that way. Then you catch another one and it suddenly turns into a dollar bill.

Two thumb sling half-dollars are needed, one to fit your left thumb and the other your right thumb, and a dollar bill. Fold the bill in half from left to right, in half again, and then from top to bottom. Have it in the left-hand pocket of your jacket. Start with the two sling coins secretly in place on your thumbs and both hands hanging naturally at your sides.

Reach up with your right hand, pretend to catch a coin from the air, thumb it into view, and hold it in front of you between your thumb and first finger. Bring your left hand up, back outward, in front of your right as if to take the coin.

As your hands come together, move your right thumb down back of its fingers to hide its coin. Bring the coin on your left thumb against the inside of your right first finger. Show it and take it away between your left thumb and first finger as you drop your right hand to your side. To the audience, it looks like the same coin, that you merely took from your right hand with your left.

Display it with your left hand and then put that hand into your pocket as if to leave it there, but draw it up behind your left thumb, immediately take that hand out of your pocket back outward, and drop it to your side.

Both hands are now at your sides as they were when you started, with a coin attached to each thumb. Repeat the same series of moves four more times, catching a coin with your right hand and apparently taking it with your left and putting it into your pocket. But as you put your left hand into your pocket the last time, really leave the coin there, by sliding your thumb out of the sling, and get the folded dollar bill into your hand. Close your fingers loosely around it, bring your hand out, and drop it to your side as before.

Reach out with your right hand to catch another coin from the air. Show it again between your thumb and finger. Bring your left hand up in front of it to take it from your right hand, but keep that hand closed around the bill it is hiding and just pretend to take the coin. Slide your right thumb behind its fingers with the coin and drop your right hand to your side.

Keep your left hand closed in front of you as if it had the coin. Then thumb the dollar bill up to the tips of those fingers to bring it into view. Turn your head and stare at it in surprise. Bring your right hand up, back outward, and take the bill with that hand, fingers in front and thumb behind it to hide the coin still on your right thumb. With your left hand, help to open out the bill, hold it displayed between both hands a moment, and then put it away into your right-hand pocket and leave the other sling coin there with it.

CONVERTIBLE HAND TUBE

You can produce, vanish, or change the color of a
handkerchief with this easily made little tube that is secretly
hidden in the hands in various ways. It can be used with or
without a bottom, can be worn on the end of the thumb, or
can be palmed from hand to hand to serve a variety of
magical uses.

What you need:
An empty bouillon-cube container. This is a small card-
board tube, about $3\frac{1}{2}''$ high and $\frac{7}{8}''$ in diameter, with a
plastic cap and metal bottom. Several different brands of
beef or chicken bouillon cubes are packaged in such tubes
and are generally available at food markets.

Flesh-colored or light-pink cloth adhesive tape, $1\frac{1}{2}''$
wide.

A razor blade in a safety holder or a sharp pointed knife.

A pencil, scissors, and a ruler.

Whatever handkerchiefs you intend to use for the various
tricks to be explained.

How you make it:
Remove the plastic cap of the bouillon tube and put it
aside for a moment. Turn the tube upside down so its closed
metal end is at the top. Measure down $1''$ from that end and
draw a pencil line around the tube. With the razor blade in
a holder or the knife, cut off the $1''$ section above the line,
the piece that includes the closed metal end, and discard it.
That gives you a tube about $2\frac{1}{2}''$ high, open at both ends.

It should be short enough to conceal within either hand
when your fingers are loosely closed in a fist around it and
the back of that hand is toward the audience. Hands vary in

size, so that if the tube is too long for your hand, use the scissors to trim it slightly shorter.

Cut off a 2½" length of the flesh-colored cloth tape. Hold the tube with its openings at the top and bottom. Fasten the tape around the tube so about ¼" of the width extends above the top end of it. Bend that extra width down over the top edge to fasten it around inside the tube. Cut another strip the same length and overlap them at the center to cover the bottom half of the tube the same way, again allowing a ¼" width to bend up over the bottom edge to the inside. The result should be that the entire outside of the tube is covered with flesh-colored tape and there are small "collars" of tape around the inside edges at both ends.

The next step is to cover the plastic cap of the tube with flesh-colored tape, but so none of it goes over the edge to the inside of the cap because that would make it too tight to fit on the tube. Cut off a 1" piece of tape, stick it to the top of the cap, and trim it off around the sides. Cut another strip 2½" long and a little more than ¼" wide and attach that around the side of the cap, but not over the bottom edge to the inside. Smooth the excess tape down over the top of the cap.

If you leave the cap off, you have a flesh-colored tube open at both ends. When you fit the cap over the bottom end, it gives you a tube with a solid bottom.

Producing a Handkerchief

You will need a silk or compressible rayon handkerchief 18" square and the tube with the cap on its bottom. Start with one diagonal corner of the handkerchief, push that down into the tube, and stuff the rest of the handkerchief in on top of it in tiny folds. Leave the last corner of the handkerchief sticking out at the top of the tube.

CONVERTIBLE HAND TUBE

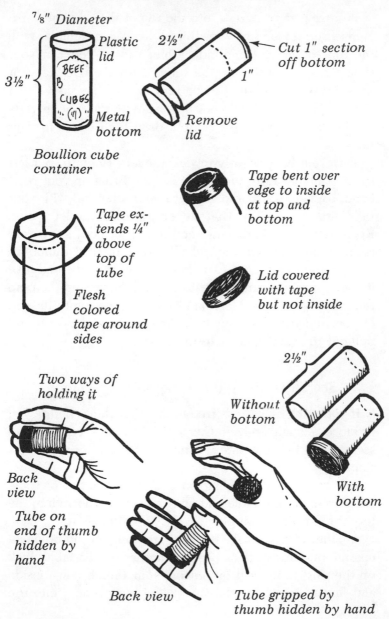

7/8" Diameter

Plastic lid

3½"

BEEF B CUBES

Metal bottom

Boullion cube container

2½"

Cut 1" section off bottom

1"

Remove lid

Tape bent over edge to inside at top and bottom

Tape extends ¼" above top of tube

Flesh colored tape around sides

Lid covered with tape but not inside

Two ways of holding it

2½"

Without bottom

With bottom

Back view

Tube on end of thumb hidden by hand

Back view

Tube gripped by thumb hidden by hand

Push your right thumb into the top of the tube until it is jammed on the end of your thumb like a big thimble, with the top corner of the handkerchief caught between your thumb and the inside of the tube. Turn the back of your hand outward and tilt the bottom end of the tube down until it is hidden behind your fingers. With the tube secretly on the end of your right thumb, drop both hands to your sides.

Turn your body slightly toward the left. Hold up your left hand, palm outward, to show it empty. Bring up your right hand, back outward, and point to your left hand with your right first finger. Tap that finger against your left palm. Keep both hands as they are and turn your body so you are facing slightly toward the right. Move your right thumb up into your left hand so it can close around the tube and take it. Lift your right hand away to show it empty and then tap the top of your closed left hand with it. Reach into the top of your left fist with your right first finger and thumb and pull out the handkerchief to display it.

Secretly Getting the Tube on Your Thumb

If you want your hands free to do other things before you produce a handkerchief, there are several ways you can secretly get the tube into position on the end of your right thumb.

You can have it standing on end behind a box or some other prop on your table and jam your thumb down into the top of the tube as you pick up the box to move it.

Another way is to have the tube standing on end inside an opaque drinking glass or plastic tumbler on the table. Pick up the glass to move it by putting your thumb down inside and fingers outside at the front. Jam your thumb into the top of the tube and lift the tube away behind your fingers as you put the glass down again.

You can also have the tube lengthwise in the right-hand pocket of your jacket. Then reach into your pocket to put away a pack of cards, a pencil, or some other small object you have been using and jam your thumb into the tube as you take your hand out again.

Simple One-hand Production

For this, instead of having the loaded tube on the end of your thumb, you hide it by secretly gripping the top end of it in the crotch of your right thumb. To position it, place the tube vertically against the palm of your right hand and close your thumb against the top of it so the top of the tube is gripped between the side of your thumb and the fleshy part of your hand just beyond the base of your first finger. Drop your hand to your side.

Face toward the left. Bring up your right hand with its back toward the audience, the tips of your fingers to the left, and your fingers spread apart. The tube, gripped by your thumb, should be entirely hidden behind the palm of your hand, and the tip of your thumb should show above the top of your hand as it normally would.

Although the audience sees only the back of your hand, your wide-open fingers give the impression that it is empty. Reach into the air once or twice as if you were trying to catch an invisible handkerchief. Close your hand into a fist around the hidden tube. Show your left hand empty, tap the top of your right hand with it, and then reach into your right fist and pull out the handkerchief.

Vanishing a Handkerchief

Have the tube and the handkerchief you intend to vanish in the left-hand pocket of your jacket. Reach into your pocket, close your fingers around the tube, and keep the back of your hand toward the audience as you take out the handkerchief.

Take the handkerchief by one corner with your right hand, shake it out and show it, then bring that hand, palm down, directly above your left fist. Gradually poke the handkerchief, a little at a time, down into your left fist and into the concealed tube. As you squeeze the last corner of the handkerchief into your fist, jam your thumb into the top of the tube.

Steal the tube away on the tip of your thumb by drawing your right hand straight up from your left fist so the tube is hidden behind your right fingers and let that hand drop to your side. Look at your closed left hand, hold it high, and then slowly open it to show that the handkerchief has disappeared.

Color Changing Handkerchief

For this, the cap is removed so that both ends of the tube are open. You will need two handkerchiefs of different colors, such as yellow and blue. Load the tube by stuffing the yellow handkerchief into it diagonally and have the loaded tube in the right-hand pocket of your jacket with the blue handkerchief.

Reach into your pocket, close your fingers around the tube to hide it, and keep the back of that hand toward the audience as you bring out the blue handkerchief. Take a corner of it with your left hand to shake it out and show it. Then take that corner between your right thumb and first finger so that the handkerchief hangs down from your right hand. Show your left hand empty and bring it in front of you, turned with its palm toward you and fingertips to the right.

Bring your right hand above your left hand and draw the handkerchief down through your left hand as the fingers of that hand close loosely around it. Pull the handkerchief straight down through the hand and away at the bottom. Do that a second time, but as your right hand comes against the palm of your slightly cupped left hand, leave the tube in your left hand as you draw the handkerchief on through. Your left hand closes loosely around the handkerchief as before and remains closed around the tube as you pull the handkerchief on through and away.

Keep your left fist closed. The blue handkerchief is still held between your right thumb and first finger as at the start. But you can now turn the palm of your right hand toward the audience to show it empty.

Do that and then bring your hand to the top of your left fist. Poke some of the blue handkerchief down into your fist and into the hidden tube. Leave the blue handkerchief there, partly sticking out of the top of your left fist, and bring your right hand under your fist. Reach up from beneath and draw a little of the yellow handkerchief into view from the bottom of the tube.

Continue to push some of the blue handkerchief into the top and pull some of the yellow handkerchief out at the bottom. The handkerchief seems to be changing color as it is pushed through your left fist. When the blue handkerchief has been pushed completely into the top and almost all the yellow one is hanging out the bottom, grip the bottom corner of the yellow handkerchief with your right first finger and thumb and pull the handkerchief down and away from your left hand.

Turn your closed left hand so the back of it is toward the floor. Immediately bring your right hand, palm down, over it to draw the handkerchief through your left. As your hands come together, steal the tube with your right hand by catching it with the tips of your fingers to press it against your palm as you continue drawing the handkerchief through your left hand and on away from it to the rear. Your left hand may now be shown empty. Your right hand, concealing the tube, displays the handkerchief that has changed from blue to yellow.

HANDKERCHIEF HANGER

This is designed for magically producing a handkerchief at your fingertips. Your hand is seen to be empty, and a moment later you reach into the air and a handkerchief appears. Several handkerchiefs may be produced that way if several of these hangers are used.

They are hidden just under the bottom edge of your jacket at either side so that when you drop your hand to your side in a natural position you can reach up underneath and secretly pull the rolled up handkerchief into your fingers. It won't unroll prematurely, but it is fixed so one corner is free. When you grip it by that corner and shake your hand, the handkerchief immediately falls open into full view.

What you need:

A pipe cleaner, the kind made of flexible wire with an absorbent covering, in the standard length of about 6".

A small safety pin.

A few ordinary straight pins.

A retractable ball-point pen.

A silk or compressible rayon handkerchief, 18" square.

How you make it:

Hold the safety pin vertically and so the clasp that opens is at the top. At the opposite end of the pin, the bottom, the wire is looped to form a small hole. Thread the pipe cleaner through the hole until half of it sticks out at each side. Then bend both ends down until they touch together for their full length.

Take the pin in your hand so the bent pipe cleaner hangs from the bottom of it. Put one corner of the handkerchief vertically *against* the top of the two wires of the pipe cleaner, just below where the pipe cleaner goes through the bottom hole of the pin. Wind the rest of the handkerchief horizontally into a compact ball by wrapping it around the outside of the pipe cleaner, but not too tightly.

When you come to the other end of the handkerchief, bring that down *between the two forks* of the pipe cleaner at the bottom. Then tuck that end up into the center of the ball of the handkerchief by pushing it in with the pen, using the end of the pen but with the point retracted so that no ink stains the handkerchief. Finally, bend the two ends of the pipe cleaner upward at each side to hold the handkerchief firmly in place.

The set-up:

Put on the jacket you intend to wear when performing. Drop your two hands to your sides. Without moving your right arm, bend only your fingers up under the bottom edge of your jacket to the inside. Where your fingers touch the lining is the proper place to pin the Handkerchief Hanger. Mark that place by pushing a straight pin through the lining there. Remove your jacket, pin the hanger and its handkerchief in place, discard the straight pin used as a marker, and put your jacket back on again.

HANDKERCHIEF HANGER

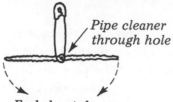

Pipe cleaner through hole

Ends bent down

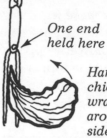

One end held here

Handkerchief wrapped around outside into a ball

Other end brought through and tucked up inside ball

Flexible wire ends of pipe cleaner bent up to hold it

Hidden under jacket

Audience

Arm at side—fingers go under edge of jacket and take handkerchief

Two or more hangers may be pinned there side by side or in a similar way under the bottom edge at the left side of your jacket, depending on how you intend to use them or how many handkerchiefs you wish to produce.

How you use it:
Show both hands empty. Turn so you are facing the right and your left side is toward the audience. Reach out with your left hand as though you were catching something from the air. Close that hand and look at it, then open it again, show it empty, and pretend to be disappointed because nothing appeared in your hand.

While you are doing that, without moving your right arm from your side, reach under the edge of your jacket with the fingers of your right hand, which is hidden by your body from the view of the audience. Grasp the rolled handkerchief *at the very top,* just beneath the pin, with your first finger at one side of the hanger and your second finger at the other side. Pull the handkerchief straight down off the hanger. That will bring the free corner of the handkerchief between those two fingers, and the handkerchief, still in a loose ball, will come off into your hand as the flexible wire of the pipe cleaner bends with the pull of your fingers and releases it.

Then turn so you are facing left and your right side is toward the audience. Reach into the air with your right hand, give your hand a little downward shake, and the handkerchief will unroll and appear hanging down from your fingertips.

While you are producing the first one with your right hand, you can secretly get a second one into your left hand from under the left side of your jacket, if you intend to produce more than one. Then turn and produce that with your left hand while your right hand secretly steals another from under its side of your jacket, and so on.

Another Way to Use It

Instead of making a trick in itself out of the production, it can be a surprising little magical incident that is part of some other trick. Say, for instance, that you need a handkerchief for some trick you are doing with a glass. Rather than simply picking up a handkerchief from your table, you reach out into the air and produce it at your fingertips, and then continue the trick with the glass.

To do that, pick up the glass with your left hand, show it and replace it on the table slightly to the right side of the table, naturally turning your body a little in that direction as you put the glass down. With your right hand at your side, reach under the edge of your jacket with your fingers, secretly get the handkerchief in that hand, and keep it concealed at your side for a moment as you face forward again. Whenever you wish, just snap out your right hand, produce the handkerchief, and go on with the trick in which it will be used.

THE BOBBY CLIPPER

This is a holder for hiding cards under the edge of your jacket so they may be added secretly to the top or bottom of a shuffled pack, to a group of cards already in your hand, or for other uses that will be explained.

What you need:
A package of bobby pins. The springy wire pins with ball tips or rubber tips that are generally used for hair setting are best. They should be about 2″ long.

Two small safety pins.

A 3″ by 5″ office index file card.

Black cloth adhesive tape, 1½" wide.
A pencil, a pair of scissors, and a ruler.
A pack of cards.

How you make it:

Cut off a 2" by 3" piece of the office index file card and discard the rest of it. Turn the piece lengthwise. Cut off two strips of the black cloth tape, each 4¼" long. Cover the front and back of the piece of card with them by fastening the strips side by side, down the front, around the bottom, and up the back to the top again.

Clip one of the bobby pins on the card by sliding it down over the top edge about 1" in from the left side. Push it all the way down until the card is entirely within the clip. Then clip a second bobby pin over the card in the same way about 1" in from the right side.

Cut off a 3" length of the cloth tape. Fasten 1" of its width lengthwise across the top of the card at the front. Bend the other ½" of its width down over the top edge and fasten it along the back. Attach a safety pin at each side of the card by pushing the pins through it from the front about ½" down from the top and ¼" in from the side.

The set-up:

Let's say you want to add the four Aces secretly to the top of a shuffled pack. Stack them together, face down, and turn them lengthwise so the narrow ends are at the sides. Slide them up under the clips of the holder, all the way up so they are held firmly. Attach the holder just above the bottom edge inside the right-hand side of your jacket, positioning it in the way that was previously explained for attaching the Handkerchief Hanger.

THE BOBBY CLIPPER

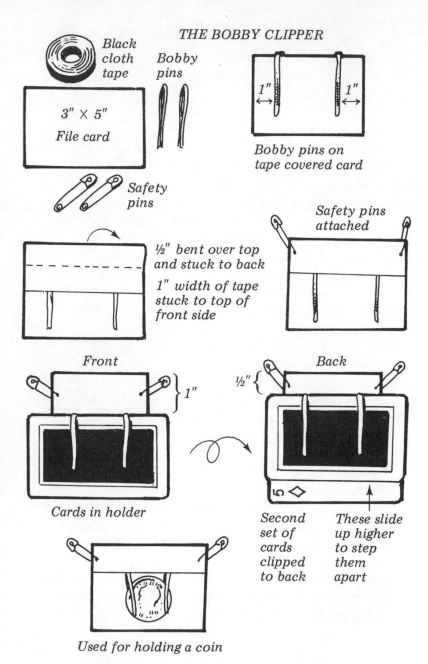

Black cloth tape

Bobby pins

3" × 5" File card

Bobby pins on tape covered card

1"   1"

Safety pins

½" bent over top and stuck to back

1" width of tape stuck to top of front side

Safety pins attached

Front

1"

Back

½"

Cards in holder

Second set of cards clipped to back

These slide up higher to step them apart

Used for holding a coin

How you use it:

After the pack has been shuffled, take it in your right hand so it lies face down across the palm of that hand, narrow ends top and bottom. Drop your right hand to your side, which naturally turns your hand and the pack so the backs of the cards are toward your side. Turn your body slightly toward the right as you speak to someone in the audience or to the person who just shuffled the cards.

As you do that, reach under your jacket with the first two fingers of your right hand, clip the cards that are in the holder between those fingers, draw them down and bring them against the top of the pack. It takes only an instant. Your arm doesn't move at all and there is very little movement of your hand.

In that way you can add not only groups of cards to a shuffled pack but a trick card or several of them to a pack that has been previously handled by the audience. If you wish to add the cards to the bottom instead of to the top of the pack, have them clipped into the holder face up instead of face down, and hold the pack face up in your hand. After you have secretly drawn them from the holder and added them to the bottom, simply tilt the pack so it lies face down in your hand.

Hiding It in Other Places

If you fasten the holder under the back edge of your jacket instead of under the side, you can add cards to a shuffled pack that has been handed to you behind your back. To do that, turn your back with your hands behind you to take the pack, then turn so you are facing front for a moment as you ask some question. Secretly add the cards from the holder and immediately turn your back again, with the pack still in your hands as it was when you took it.

By pinning the holder just below the inside pocket of your jacket at either side, you can secretly add cards to a pack in your hand as you reach into your jacket to take a pencil, an envelope, or something else from that pocket.

Using It As a Double Holder

The Bobby Clipper will hold two separate packets of cards. Slide a few cards under the clips at the front and then turn it over to the back. Slide a second set of cards under the clips at the back. You will see that because of the way the tape has been fastened across the top of the holder those cards don't go up as far under the clips as the cards did at the front.

It is designed that way so the two packets are not only kept apart by the holder but one set is stepped ¼″ below the other. You can tell by a touch of your fingers which is which and instantly draw either packet from under the edge of your jacket to secretly add various cards to the pack as they are needed for some particular trick.

Using It with Other Things

The Bobby Clipper will also serve as a good holder for a coin of half-dollar size, or for two coins if one is fastened under the back set of clips and the other under the front set.

It will hold a key, a folded dollar bill, a small slip of paper upon which something has been written, or a pay envelope that you may wish to add to a stack of envelopes in your hand.

TIP-OVER COIN HOLDER

This will deliver eight coins of half-dollar size into your hand for the trick of catching coins from the air or for whatever other magical use you may make of them. It holds them securely until they are wanted and slides them out into your cupped hand from beneath the edge of your jacket in a way that eliminates fumbling with catches, clamps, or other mechanical devices.

What you need:
An empty pocket matchbox, the cardboard kind with a cover and sliding drawer.
A small safety pin, about 1″ long.
Black cloth adhesive tape, ¾″ wide.
Eight coins of half-dollar size.
A pencil, scissors, and a ruler.

How you make it:
Remove the drawer of the matchbox and put that aside for a moment. Put the matchbox cover lengthwise on a table, measure in 1½″ from the left end of it, and draw a vertical pencil line across it. Cut off that end of the cover, right across the top, sides, and bottom, and discard the rest of the cover.

Take a strip of the black cloth tape 3½″ long and fasten it from one side of that piece of the matchbox cover across the bottom end and up the other side. Smooth it down along the edges. You now have what amounts to a little box with an open top and with a bottom closed off with tape.

Cut one end off the *drawer* of the matchbox, which will give you a piece of cardboard about 1¼″ long and slightly less than ½″ wide. With the point of the scissors, push that small piece of cardboard down inside the little box made from the matchbox cover until it is flat at the bottom of it. That reinforces the taped bottom and covers the sticky surface of the tape inside the bottom.

The safety pin must now be fastened to one end of a strip of black tape 3½″ long. Cut off a strip of tape that length. Hold the pin lengthwise, with the pin part at the top, the bar at the bottom, and so the clasp is to the left and the looped hinge of the pin to the right. Open the pin and lay one end of the tape over the bottom bar of it so that you can bend about ½″ of the end of the tape over the bar and stick it against the tape at the other side. Press the tape together so the pin is firmly held at that end of it.

Rest the little box on the table so its narrow ends are top and bottom. Take the tape to which the pin is attached and fasten *the other end* of it vertically to the outside face of the box at its center, from the bottom straight up. About 1½″ of the tape will extend straight up above the top of the box to the pin attached to its far end.

Turn the box over to its other side. You will see that the part of the tape between the pin and the top of the box has a sticky surface exposed. That should be covered by fastening another strip of tape to it. Use a strip about 2½″ long, stick the two together so their sticky surfaces meet, and then fasten the remainder of that strip down inside the box.

Complete the construction by covering the entire outside of the box with black tape, by fastening overlapping horizontal strips around it, but don't bend any of those over to the inside.

The set-up:

The Tip-over Coin Holders may be worn at either side, just above the bottom inside edge of your jacket, positioned in the same way as the other holders. But they must be pinned in a special way to work properly.

For explanation, let's say that you are going to wear one of the holders under the right-hand side of your jacket. Put the eight coins into it and then rest it on a table so it is standing upright on its bottom. Now turn it so the side with the pin and tape is toward the left. Keep it turned that way and fasten it with the pin to the inside lining of your jacket at the right-hand side, in proper position so that it will be hidden just above your hand when you drop your hand to that side.

Whether it is pinned under the right or left side of your jacket, *the side of the holder to which the hanging tape is attached should always be toward your body.*

How you use it:

With the loaded holder pinned in place, drop your right hand to your side and momentarily turn your body to the right so your left side is toward the audience. Without moving your arm, cup your hand under the edge of your jacket until the tips of your fingers touch the bottom of the little box. Slowly push it in toward your body and tip it up and over far enough so the coins quietly slide out of the top of the box and right into your hand. Keep your fingers loosely curled around them as you withdraw your hand from under the edge of your jacket. With your arm still hanging naturally at your side, turn so you are facing front again.

Catching Coins from the Air

If you wish to use the eight coins for a simple production of them from the air, reach out with the back of your hand toward the audience, the coins concealed in the curled fingers of that hand. Put your thumb against the face of the

TIPOVER COIN HOLDER

Cardboard pocket matchbox cover and drawer

Cover cut to get 1½" section

End covered with tape

Makes small box

Pin

Tape laid over bar of pin

Back

½" of tape bent over

Tape extends ½" above top

Pin fastened to tape

Tape with pin fastened to back of box

Box covered with black tape

Coins inside

Other side

Second strip stuck to first goes down into box

Finished holder

Pinned to inside of jacket

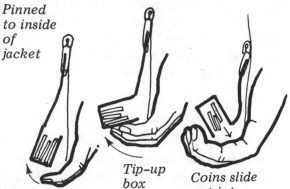

This side toward body

Fingers come under

Tip-up box

Coins slide out into cupped hand

top coin of the stack and slide it upward against the inside of your fingers until you bring it into view between your thumb and first finger.

Hold that coin there long enough for the audience to see it. Turn your left hand palm upward and drop the coin into that hand. With your right hand, reach to your left elbow, pretend to pluck a coin from there, and thumb another one up into view. Show that and drop it into your left hand. Then pretend to pull a coin from behind your right knee, and so on until you have produced them all, one at a time. Finally pour the coins from hand to hand and then take them all in your right hand and spill them out of your hand across your table.

For a more elaborate production, two coin holders can be used, one pinned under each side of your jacket, so that you can produce a number of coins first with one hand and then the other.

INDEX